SHERPA

• • • • •

SHERPA

· · · · · ·

THE MEMOIR OF ANG THARKAY

BY ANG THARKAY

WITH BASIL P. NORTON

Foreword by
TASHI SHERPA

Afterword by
DAWA SHERPA

Translated from the French by
CORINNE McKAY

LEGENDS AND LORE SERIES

MOUNTAINEERS
BOOKS

MOUNTAINEERS BOOKS

Mountaineers Books is the publishing division of The Mountaineers, an organization founded in 1906 and dedicated to the exploration, preservation, and enjoyment of outdoor and wilderness areas.

1001 SW Klickitat Way, Suite 201, Seattle, WA 98134
800.553.4453, www.mountaineersbooks.org

Original French-language edition *Mémoires d'un Sherpa* published by Amiot-Dumont
© 1954 by *Le Livre Contemporain, Amiot-Dumont*
English-language translation © 2016 Corinne McKay
Foreword © 2016 by Tashi Sherpa
Afterword © 2016 by Dawa Sherpa

Printed in the United States of America
19 18 17 16 1 2 3 4 5

Copy editor: Chris Dodge
Layout: Jen Grable
Series design: Karen Schober
Cartographer: Marge Mueller, Gray Mouse Graphics
Cover photograph: *Ang Tharkay on Mount Everest Expedition, 1935* © Royal Geographical Society
Frontispiece: *Ang Tharkay on Mount Everest Reconnaissance Expedition, 1951* © Royal Geographical Society

Library of Congress Cataloging-in-Publication Data
Names: Tharkay, Ang, 1907-1981. | Norton, Basil P.
Title: Sherpa : the memoir of Ang Tharkay / by Ang Tharkay, with Basil P. Norton ; foreword by
 Tashi Sherpa ; afterword by Dawa Sherpa ; translated from the French by Corinne McKay.
Other titles: Memoires d'un Sherpa. English
Description: Seattle, WA : Mountaineers Books, [2016] | Series: Legends and
 Lore | "Original French-language edition Memoires d'un Sherpa published by
 Amiot-Dumont ?1954 by Le Livre Contemporain, Amiot-Dumont"—T.p. verso.
Identifiers: LCCN 2015034050| ISBN 9781594859977 (trade paper) | ISBN 9781594859984 (ebook)
Subjects: LCSH: Tharkay, Ang, 1907-1981. | Mountaineering guides (Persons)—Himalaya
 Mountains—Biography. | Mountaineering—Himalaya Mountains—History.
Classification: LCC GV199.92.T5 A32513 2016 | DDC 796.552092-dc23
LC record available at http://lccn.loc.gov/2015034050

Mountaineers Books titles may be purchased for corporate, educational, or other promotional sales, and our authors are available for a wide range of events. For information on special discounts or booking an author, contact our customer service at 800-553-4453 or mbooks@mountaineersbooks.org.

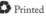 Printed on recycled paper

ISBN (paperback): 978-1-59485-997-7
ISBN (ebook): 978-1-59485-998-4

CONTENTS

Foreword: Sirdar Nonpareil by Tashi Sherpa7
Introduction to the original edition by Basil P. Norton11

Part I: Childhood and First Expeditions
1. My Childhood 21
2. Travels to Tibet. 29
3. Sherpa Country and Its Inhabitants 33
4. I Choose a Career as a Sherpa 45
5. My Expeditions to Everest. 53

Part II: Other Expeditions
1. My First Expedition to Nanda Devi 83
2. Kabru. 91
3. My Second Expedition to Nanda Devi 95
4. My First Journey to the Karakoram 99
5. My Second Expedition to the Karakoram109

Part III: Annapurna
1. My First Contact with the French Expedition.117
2. En Route. .121
3. Reconnaissance.127
4. The Assault .135
5. Victory .139

6. The Return . 143
7. A Week in Paris 153

Epilogue: Nun Kun 161
Praise and Testimonials 167
Afterword by Dawa Sherpa 175
Acknowledgments for the original edition, 1954 177
Acknowledgments for the new edition 177
Expedition History Summary 179
Notes . 181
Bibliography . 191
Index . 201

List of Maps

Area map with Country of the Sherpas detail 16
Nanda Devi Massif 82
The Karakoram . 108
Annapurna . 116

MAP KEY

● capital ▬ ▪ ▬ border

● town or village ☀ glacier

▲ peak +++++++ railroad

Foreword: Sirdar Nonpareil

My lasting image of Agu (Uncle) Tharkay focuses on his broad grin—sparkling and endearing—and his dense wave of dark hair. Agu Tharkay radiated warmth, seemed impervious to envy, and instantly made one feel safe in his presence. I can't remember him ever not smiling.

Even as an eight-year-old I knew, from the banter among us cousins, of his special status. This status was burnished by our hero worship and reinforced by how my other uncles and the *mikarus* (foreigners) deferred to him as a person and as a mountaineer. The Sherpas affectionately accorded him a pedestal, as only cohorts who have prevailed through the same gauntlet of ice and snow would do. We reveled in his prowess as a climber, respected his wisdom as a sirdar, and marveled at how the legendary European climbers praised the "great-hearted Ang Tharkay" in their own epic tales. He was an equal in an exclusive club with Shipton, Tilman, Herzog, Hillary, and of course Tenzing Norgay. India's most famous climber, M. S. Kohli, honored him as "the king amongst the Sherpas." He was *the* Sherpa before Tenzing became the beacon of hope in a world still recovering from the ravages of war.

Himalayan mountaineering in the early thirties was fraught with peril and very little reward. Beside the unpredictable avalanches and crevasses that killed and maimed many, frostbite was the common enemy. But that did not prevent climbers from reaching 28,000 feet, which at that time was the highest point any human had reached. Expedition members went through

an arduous two-month trek through the forbidding Tibetan Plateau, and then up the difficult North Col, often without supplemental oxygen and with equipment that would be considered suicidal today.

Tibet was then closed and shrouded in mystery for Westerners, and little was known to them about its neighbor, Nepal. The lure of Shangri-La, of mysterious, hidden peaks and valleys, was great, and a race began between Europe's elite explorers which would continue for more than two decades. That era of swashbuckling mountaineering in the twenties and thirties coincided with the discovery of the Sherpa as a trustworthy, hardy companion on the treacherous slopes of the Karakoram and the Himalayas. The legend of the Sherpa as indefatigable and indispensable on the mountains was passed by word of mouth and written up in copious field reports by adventurers seeking discoveries and first summits, some for themselves, and others for the glory of waning empires.

History tells us that the first Sherpas came from Tibet and settled in the isolated high reaches of Nepal's mountains. Life offered few choices. A young man either became a yak herder for the family or joined the monk-hood. The land yielded little, so many looked far beyond the crags and rivers of the Khumbu valley in search of a better future. Darjeeling, a resort town in British India, teeming with itinerant traders, soldiers, and civil servants seeking recreation, was the hub for many such youths who sought work and a steady income. Mountaineering seemed to be a natural choice for those who had lived their whole lives in the sacred shadow of a towering peak they called Chomolungma.

The early Sherpas never sought fame. They ventured into perilous zones of hitherto unexplored ranges, ate food that was strange to them, and met and worked with strangers who would become lifelong admirers of the Sherpas' bravery, grit, and loyalty. They rallied back to their worried families, just happy to be alive and sometimes satisfied knowing that their best efforts had helped the "sahibs" in the success of an expedition. They risked their lives for a few rupees and the promise of a job for another season. That is what Ang Tharkay and his friends did in the early years.

It does not matter which book of climbing history you choose. The story reads the same. By mid-century, Sherpas were integral to the lore

of mountaineering, and their reputation continued to grow within climbing circles. Then one morning, in May 1953, the whole world woke up to learn that the highest summit on the planet had been climbed. Soon they would see the photograph of a climber, with ice ax raised, on the top of the world—an image now etched forever as a glorious exclamation of triumph over nature. And it happened to be a Sherpa up there.

This moment had actually been decades in the making. The Sherpas in the thirties had first been recruited as porters or coolies, but expedition members had rapidly discovered that they could do a lot more than just carry heavy loads up steep slopes. These men could climb higher and acclimatize much faster than anyone. But that was not all. Time and again, the Sherpas went beyond perceived limits. They became indispensable lieutenants, cultural liaisons (protecting expeditions' resources from extortionate locals), climbing partners, and fearless rescuers in times of crisis. Time and again, expedition leaders found themselves moved beyond words to describe Sherpa ingenuity.

Tenzing standing atop Everest must have been the turning point. A shift took place in mountaineering perspective. Now almost anyone who wanted to climb or explore the Himalayas needed to call on the group of people who proudly called themselves Sherpas. All of them, whether they acknowledged it or not, were indebted to Ang Tharkay and a legion of unsung compatriots who had climbed before them, whose amazing ability and valor provided the Sherpas their base and their inspiration.

In the decades that followed, new generations of mountaineering Sherpas continued the legacy of their forebears with remarkable fortitude. Success came to many who braved the dangers of the Himalayas, and a slew of super-Sherpas have built their own fame. But this has come with a high cost. More than 250 Sherpas have died in the quest to reach the summit and to help others reach it, and the risks don't seem to decrease, as evidenced by the death toll in recent years.

The role and the reward for the ordinary Sherpa porter has not changed much over the years. He is still expected to take most of the risks, lay the ropes, carry heavy loads up and down the treacherous icefalls, and face the rage of the mountain. Sadly, the inequity in the business of climbing hasn't

changed much over the years, either. Eighty years ago a Sherpa's frostbitten finger was valued at ten rupees, and a life lost on the mountains paid no more than one thousand. The numerical payout may have since increased, but the true value of a Sherpa porter's life is still grossly undervalued.

Climbing on Everest today is no longer such an exclusive endeavor, provided one has money and time. Despite its dangers, it sometimes seems no more than a bucket-list item for rush-seeking clients looking ahead to a selfie on the summit. Still, nostalgia for a long-gone era colors my perspective. I have never been a climber, but I have lived close to many of them and inhaled the precious air of their stories on the slopes. Listening to these accounts, I could hear the ice crunch under crampons and feel the icy bite of the wind in a lonely tent on Camp III. I was not there—but I *was* there with Agu Tharkay, Agu Da Namgyal, Agu Pasang Phutar, and Agu Tenzing.

I often wonder what Agu Tharkay would have to say about this new age of mountaineering. Would he still smile his blessings because so many after him have achieved new glories on the path his generation blazed so painstakingly? Would he finally feel rewarded? Or would he guide them to another route for another calling?

I hope that his memoirs will guide me to my answer.

Tashi Sherpa
July 2015

Note: To be true to the original, we have not corrected obvious mistakes, including errors in geography, elevation, etc., on the maps and in the text. While for reasons of legibility and quality of reproduction we have redrawn the maps, we have done so faithfully, errors and all.

—Mountaineers Books

Introduction to the Original Edition by Basil P. Norton

It is often difficult to explain how things happen. I absolutely never expected to be writing a Sherpa's life story, until Ang Tharkay came to see me.[1]

When he came to ask me to do this, I had just been looking out my window at the sparkling peak of Kanchenjunga, and I was trying to imagine what people might feel and experience in those mountains that are as inaccessible as they are mesmerizing. One might even say that Ang Tharkay was sent as a messenger by the imposing mountains whose silhouettes I could see in the distance, as if revealing their hidden wonders to me.

As soon as we sat down to discuss the process, I found Ang Tharkay to be a charming and modest man. He was simple and unpretentious, but he had a tough spirit and loved to take risks. We became fast friends, and soon we were starting to write his life story.

The biggest obstacle was language. Ang Tharkay spoke only a little English, and I knew only a few words in Nepali. We both spoke Hindi, but neither one of us spoke it well enough to translate our thoughts into fluent English. In the end, we used an interpreter who spoke both Nepali and English. Happily, we had a mutual friend: Mohan Lal Mukerjee, who knew both languages and agreed to transcribe Ang Tharkay's story in English as he was speaking.

Afterward, I simply referred to the notes that Mohan Lal Mukerjee had laboriously recorded, and to Ang Tharkay's faithful memories. But there were difficulties when I had to transform these compelling, disjointed stories into a book that was faithful to the truth but also readable.

Ang Tharkay never worked as anything other than a Sherpa, and he doesn't aspire to any kind of literary fame. He was content with the rough, honest life that his people lived, and despite the attention that his climbing achievements had brought him, he didn't want to present himself as a writer in any way.

But his modesty and lack of pretention never kept him from being passionately in love with the mountains, even when he worked as a porter, a cook, or a supervisor for the coolies. In the various expeditions that he joined, he wasn't in any way interested in scientific technique or spectacular exploits: the only thing he wanted was to be of service to the "sahibs," to help them in their audacious attempts to conquer the dangerous giants of the Himalayas, and to rejoice in their successes as if they were his own.[2] His sense of service and his kindness earned him high praise. The diary of every expedition he worked for mentions this. His inexhaustible loyalty and devotion and his spirit of cooperation were most appreciated.

He was the acknowledged leader of his own team of Sherpas. His men loved, respected, and obeyed him. All it took was a word from Ang Tharkay to bring them running, and no expedition leader would have made any important decision without consulting him. If a Sherpa had complaints about a sahib, Ang Tharkay was always asked to resolve the dispute. He did this with so much tact and intelligence that soon everyone was laughing and there was no trace of conflict. His personality was such that he got along equally well with the sahibs and the other Sherpas, and this allowed him to resolve many unpleasant situations. Many times his quick work saved a climber from serious, even fatal injuries. He was a tender, sympathetic nurse for anyone who had snow blindness or frostbite, he was an intrepid rescuer and a true friend when danger arose, and he never dwelled for a moment on his own safety or the risks he was taking.

However, he had some shortcomings. He was often very upset about a minor incident that he took to heart, as if it were an insult to his personal

dignity. He didn't always understand the European ways of doing things, and he reacted very strongly if he felt that he was being treated as an underling. He was scrupulous to a fault when it came to managing provisions, and he was too meticulous about salvaging the food that was inevitably wasted. But his incredible assets far outweighed his minor shortcomings, and during expeditions he was unanimously seen as one of the most useful, confident, and loyal Sherpa leaders that anyone could ever want.

In looking through the published reports of various Himalayan expeditions, I was surprised to find so many references to the role that Ang Tharkay played, and to read such high praise about him. This made me realize how well known and sought-after he was by all of the Himalayan experts. Over the course of many years, he participated in nearly every [Himalayan] expedition that climbers from any country embarked on. This earned him a reputation as an indispensable colleague. The recent American expedition to Makalu insisted on hiring him, and despite how attached he was to this biography project, Ang Tharkay couldn't resist accepting their offer.[3]

With the exception of Tenzing Norgay, who has since risen to fame after conquering Everest with Hillary, no other Sherpa has ever known this kind of recognition.

Ang Tharkay's great renown is due particularly to his heroic service on Annapurna, which was truly the apex of his career. On Annapurna, he gave the best of himself and was lauded by Maurice Herzog, the courageous and heroic leader of the French expedition. Ang Tharkay became a lifelong friend of Herzog, who wrote an unforgettable story of Himalayan climbing. During their tragic return journey, Ang Tharkay poured all of his experience and devotion into caring for members of the French expedition who were suffering terribly.

This book makes no claims beyond being an autobiography of Ang Tharkay, but my own inexperience with the literary technique that needed to be used required that I transcend those boundaries. Ang Tharkay told his stories in real time, in his native language, so I had to read many books about the Himalayas to learn about the places in his stories. I used a number of primary sources and much of my own technical documentation and geographic descriptions, people's names, and details about trip itineraries

and schedules. At the top of my list are two books by Eric Shipton: *Upon That Mountain* and *Mount Everest Reconnaissance Expedition, 1951*. I could not have written the chapters on the Karakoram and Nanda Devi without the technical and geographical details that I found in those books. H. W. Tilman's *Everest 1938* and Hugh Ruttledge's *Everest 1933* were a great help in retracing Ang Tharkay's numerous expeditions in the Everest region. Maurice Herzog's *Annapurna* was my guidebook for the entire third section, with the exception of the last chapter.

The first part of this book is specifically devoted to the stories that Ang Tharkay told me about his childhood and his first experiences on Everest. This is probably the first story of its kind. I have known many Himalayan explorers, obsessive athletes who can talk of nothing but their climbs. They are always hunting for new adventures and new expeditions. In these climbers' eyes, Ang Tharkay was one of a kind. For better or worse, he was their hero. They were constantly after him, to have the benefit of his experience. For them, his biography will hold a powerful interest.

Sherpa country is mysterious and remote, hidden in the heart of the mighty Himalayas, at the foot of the mind-boggling peaks of the Everest massif. It is not a wealthy area, and the people who live there are humble mountain peasants. Their lives are far removed from those of their neighbors in the valleys and on the plains, where life is easier. They are under Nepal's administrative control, but they have so little contact with the outside world that the government in Kathmandu sees little benefit in "civilizing" this region. The only contact that these people have with the outside world is in their modest "capital city"—Namche Bazaar, where a low-level Nepali civil servant presides over their administrative aspects. Having no other way to earn a meager living, they till their fields, raise livestock, and ask only to participate in the many international expeditions in the Himalayas as guides, porters, and cooks. In that way, they have earned a much-deserved reputation as an indispensable part of every Himalayan expedition.

Everyone who reads this book must be prepared to climb the Himalayas, not with the expert climbers on the major expeditions, but with the anonymous, courageous local mountain people who carry the foreign climbers' supplies and equipment, with the helpers who set up the tents, and with the

staff and cooks who prepare the climbers' food and serve it to them. Those are the tasks that fall to the Sherpas in the land of eternal snow, ice, and constant avalanche danger. The Sherpas are skilled at hiring coolies along the route and at resolving their disputes, soothing their grievances, watching over camp fires, preparing hot meals, making sure that the insatiable stoves are always supplied with scarce fuel, and scouring villages and nomad camps for supplies of meat and fresh produce. These tasks are not in any way secondary. On the contrary, an expedition's success depends on them. Ang Tharkay performed those tasks, and every expedition leader he served thanked him profusely.

This is a sincere, unaltered story told by an unsophisticated mountain man, whose singular passion was to follow the Himalayan explorers in their attempts to conquer the world's highest peaks.

AREA MAP WITH COUNTRY OF THE SHERPAS DETAIL (as represented in the original 1954 book)

T I B E T

TENGKEY DZONG

KHAMBA DZONG

B

Siri

Muk

Gompa

Dong Kung

Thanggu

T

28°

BHUTAN

Lachen

Phari Dzong

KABRU
7338 m

SIKKIM

Gautsa

Singalila

Yatung

Jelep-La

GANGTOK Natu-La
BAGLUNG 4267 m

EVEREST
8840 m

Cnola Khola

NUPTSE
7827

LHOTSE
8500 m

Richingpong Singtam

Phalut

Rhenok

ARKANGE
6446 m

Dudh Kosi

Terhathum

Kalimpong

TAWECHE
6520 m

Pheriche

DARJEELING

Imja Khola

Singalapa

Ilam Simina

Bhote Kosi

Pangboche

AMA-DABLAM
6800 m

Khunde Porchi

Thame Khumjung

Tenboche

Thami Khola

Namche Bazaar

KANGTEGA
6809 m

27°45′

THAMSERKU
6623 m

K H U M B U

Dudh Kosi

Hongu Khola

A

Taksindhou

86°45′

**Detail: The Country
of the Sherpas**

KILOMETERS

0 1 2 3 4 5 10

88°

89°

88°

PART I

· · · · · ·

CHILDHOOD AND
FIRST EXPEDITIONS

| I |

MY CHILDHOOD

I WAS BORN IN THE village of Khunde, in the year Ta-Lak-Te, the Tibetan Year of the Monkey,[1] 1907 on the Christian calendar. My village is near the Tengboche Monastery, in a valley in the Khumbu region. It is part of the Solu-Khumbu subregion of eastern Nepal. As part of the Nepali district of Okhaldhunga, Solu-Khumbu is inhabited entirely by Sherpas, which has earned it the name "Country of the Sherpas."

Khunde is too small to be found on any map, and the population is fairly spread out. It is in the very heart of the Himalayas at an altitude of about 4000 meters. Surrounded by high peaks, it is isolated from the rest of the world.

I am the oldest in my family.[2] My mother, being delicately built, had a very difficult birth with me.

My parents were married in Khunde, but my mother was from Olung, about thirty kilometers from Shekar Dzong,[3] across the Tibetan border. Their marriage was the epilogue to a love story that began just after my mother was forced to flee from her village after clashing with its leader. She walked all the way to Khunde, a difficult journey that took her six days. There she met my father, and he took her to his parents' house. They took her in, and the wedding was planned for that year.

My father had a younger brother, so he could not lay claim to the family's property. In Sherpa families it is customary that the youngest child inherits the parents' estate.[4] So my father's brother inherited the family property, and my father was left to fend for himself as best he could. When my grandfather died, my uncle took possession of my grandparents' land and house, and he still lives there today.

But at that time, my father was able to purchase one of our neighbors' houses. This neighbor had no family and so decided to enter a monastery. He agreed to turn over his house as long as my father paid the yearly taxes. This was a favorable arrangement and a real stroke of luck for my father. It saved him a great deal of worry and trouble. We had no money or possessions, and it seemed that God had wanted to save us from poverty by giving us a house on such favorable terms. We moved in immediately, and my two youngest brothers were born there.

Our house was a single story. Its walls were built of rough stone and the roof was made of wooden planks. With two small rooms, it was just big enough for all of us. Our entire family lived in one room, and we used the other as a stable for our animals. As with all of the houses in our region, it faced east so that the first rays of the rising sun would provide the warmth that we needed to start the day.

My father was poor, even by the standards of a village where no one was rich. He had trouble providing even the basics for his large family. So, when my aunt offered for me to come live with her, my father agreed immediately.

She lived in Da-Te, a small village just over the Tibetan border. I was filled with excitement at the idea of traveling, and I loved the journey that my aunt and I took by mule. I immediately felt a connection with my aunt. She was a wonderful woman, and we quickly became very attached. She was single and had no children, so she was looking for someone to love. I was about six years old, and she soon became like a second mother to me. She never failed to bring back a present for me when she went to the bazaar: a treat, a toy, or something to wear. I still remember that sometimes when she left me home alone, I could not stop crying and calling for her. I was terrified of being abandoned, with only her two mean black cows for company. Only when she came home and gathered me in her arms did I feel reassured and

happy again. The days that I spent at her house were among the happiest of my childhood, and I will never forget them.

I had lived with my aunt for six years when my father came to see us, and he said that he wanted to bring me back home. The separation was harsh, and I cried bitterly when I left my second mother. But my parents needed me, and I knew that it was my duty to go back to their house. I was their oldest son, and at twelve years old it was time for me to work a bit for them.

There was no lack of work at home. I was responsible for watching over the goats and cows, taking them out to pasture, keeping an eye on them, and bringing them back to their stable at night. I spent every day wandering over hills and mountains with them, walking along rushing streams and steep-sided valleys. I remember that the Tengboche monastery was being built then, and I spent more than one day watching villagers carry stone blocks there for the Tibetan stonemasons to chisel down to size. I was interested in their work, and I listened to them talk or sing while they worked, as was their custom. That monastery is still well-known among travelers and pilgrims. My youngest brother, Ang Phutar, who often went walking with me, stayed in Khunde with my parents.[5] He was their heir and would inherit their estate after they died. He managed their property, took care of their affairs, and in general saw to their needs as they got older.

We had to subsist on the land we owned, three or four acres of tortured soil where we grew a few plots of potatoes, turnips, and carrots, in addition to the black wheat that is the staple in our region. We used the wheat flour for our bread, and we filled out our diet with vegetables and milk. We produced just enough to feed ourselves, and if we ever had an exceptional harvest, we offered the surplus to our neighbors.

When my father was able to save a little money, he used it to travel to Tibet to buy wool or salt crystals. We brought these supplies back home, partly for our own use and partly to trade them for rice, which we usually kept for festivals and holidays. In our area rice is a luxury and is sold for a high price. Sometimes we went to Jayanagar to buy saffron and molasses. And if we could buy a large amount of wool, we used the leftovers to make blankets and carpets. We were even able, little by little, to set up a small business selling wool, and I started making frequent trips to Tibet with my

father. I will talk about these trips later, but they went on for several years, and through them I came to know Tibet and its residents more deeply.

I went to Jayanagar and Kosisagar for the great bazaar or *mela* (fair) that happens once each year in the month of Magh (mid-February).

I usually went away for a week or two. I soon gained considerable experience along the route and at the markets. While I was gone, my mother and my younger siblings did my regular work at home. But as soon as my brothers were old enough, they came along with me, and before long they could take my place on the trips. Then I had enough time to help my father with his other jobs.

When we went to cold places, we wore special footwear called *dochas*, a kind of high boot or legging made of untanned leather. They were stuffed with dried straw to protect our legs from the dampness and cold. These boots are what all of the Sherpas usually wear while trekking. In every village, making dochas is truly an industry, and the artisans who sell them for between two and four-and-a-half rupees per pair do very good business.

We wore our hair in long braids that we wrapped around our heads like a kind of turban. My mother always rubbed her hair with butter when she combed it, a Tibetan custom that we also adopted.

Unlike most people from our region, my father was a scrupulous non-drinker. He didn't like *chang* (a locally made beer) or other alcoholic drinks. He was a calm and reserved man with unsophisticated tastes. He never took part in discussions or arguments, and he never intervened in fights. He was well built, robustly healthy, and he loved to travel, hunt, and climb. My mother was more social and liked everything that her friends in the village liked. Most Sherpa women get drunk from time to time, and my mother was no exception. At home we brewed a kind of beer from dried corn. It has a bit of a bite but is not very alcoholic and gets you only a little tipsy.

While my father didn't drink, he was a heavy smoker, too much so for my mother, who was nauseated by the smell of tobacco more than by the sight of my father smoking. She made such a scene with my father about it that he was reduced to sneaking around behind her back. Although he swore to the gods that he would never smoke again, the vice had him in its clutches.

One day we were walking to the bazaar together, and my father took out his tobacco to roll a cigarette. I reminded him of the promise that he had made to my mother. He answered that he was doing his best to quit smoking and that this cigarette would be his last. But a little farther along he rolled another one, and I realized that he would never be free of his passion. I searched helplessly for whatever radical solution I could find to cure him, and I resolved to trick him by rolling a cigarette filled with tobacco and a little bit of ground hot pepper. When he lit it, he was overcome with a horrible fit of coughing, and I ran away for fear that he would give me a well-deserved punishment. But fortunately for me he didn't lose his temper. He called to me and congratulated me, laughing, for the sly trick that I had played on him, but he warned me that this method had little chance of convincing him to quit. I felt terrible about the cruel thing that I had done, and I humbly asked him to forgive me. Although my father had taken the whole thing as a joke, I will never forget that incident. If I can admit this, it saved me from a love of tobacco.

For us, finding water was a major problem. Although Khunde had a fountain, we sometimes had to go collect water from the neighboring village's well, nearly two kilometers away. My mother had to carry it in a wooden bucket called a *shee-shom*, which could hold about forty liters. In the winter, it was very hard to draw water from the well because the surface was usually covered with a thick layer of ice that we had to crack. We used this water for everything: drinking, washing, and for our livestock.

In the winter it was so cold that to store our potatoes, carrots, and other vegetables, we had to bury them in a pit that was two or two-and-a-half meters deep. Besides black wheat, our staples were corn and buckwheat, which, after they were ground, we stored in wooden crates or leather pouches.

When I was thirteen years old, a few months after I returned home from living with my aunt, I participated in my first ritual celebration: *Losar* (Tibetan New Year). My father was gravely ill at that time, due to an accident that he'd had in the forest while chopping wood. His axe had slipped and severely injured his leg. Then he had come down with a fever, complicated by bronchitis, and he had to stay in bed for nearly six months. My mother took care of him tenderly and patiently, for that entire time. I remember that

the festival fell during December. It was a very harsh winter, and my mother had given me a goatskin coat that she had made, because she could not allow herself the luxury of buying one. At that time, we were in very dire straits and had great difficulty getting enough food to stave off hunger. But for the festival, it is customary to offer rice to one's guests, so we absolutely had to find a way to get some.

I was sent to Oaku, a village inhabited by the neighboring tribe, the Rai. It was just on the edge of the Khumbu, and they grew rice there. We had to borrow salt from our neighbors and trade it for rice, but the amount that we got was not enough, and the festival date was approaching. Fortunately my father was getting better little by little, and finally he was able to go to Oaku himself. He was well known there, and he was able to buy the rice that we needed on credit. My father even brought me back a wool suit that I wore for the festival. Thus we were able to show that we could meet our obligations.

But with all of that, we built up a heavy burden of debt, which worsened our already straitened situation. I was obliged to go and work for other people as a cowherd, a woodcutter, and a day laborer so that I could add a meager amount to my family's income.

Summer came and I was sent to a village between Khunde and Tengboche, to cut hay for a relative of my father. As it was quite hot, I took off my handsome suit and lay it down in the field. At the end of the day, I found that someone had stolen it.

A week later, I was sent to take some chauri cows (a cross between Tibetan yak and Indian cow) out to pasture at an altitude of 4500 to 4800 meters. At that altitude it was bitterly cold at night, and I had absolutely nothing to cover up with. I was able to get a *chuk-tuk* (a type of Tibetan carpet made of raw wool), and I had a sort of rough coat made from it. But it was so full of lice that the insect bites made me forget the warmth that the coat offered. I hired out my services throughout the area, and it wasn't until two years later that I was able to return home and back to my usual jobs.

When I was eighteen, I came down with severe dysentery, and I lost a lot of blood so I had to stay in bed. This epidemic disease devastated many villages, all the way to Namche Bazaar, and I must have caught it from a

villager who came to see us one day and was also sick with it. I was left alone, and our friends would not enter our house. I will always be grateful to my mother for taking care of me with endless tenderness and attention.

Thus went my childhood. I crossed the high country of our isolated Himalayan region from every direction, and everywhere and always I saw the snow-covered high peaks. I gained a respect for them that verged on adoration for the gods that ruled over our little world. We were forbidden to try to seek them out, to try to visit their sanctuaries. At that time, I never thought that my future career would force me to go against my childhood faith.

I knew nothing of the outside world, and I was perfectly content with my lot as a peasant. Because there was no school in our region, my ignorance did not bother me, and I drifted along in this existence with no goals or desires until the day when destiny took me to Darjeeling. My father had sent me there for some reason that I have since forgotten.

I arrived in that magnificent mountain town in May, the time of year when it is at its most beautiful and there are throngs of visitors from every part of India as well as other countries. For me, it was the discovery of a new world. I found myself immersed in the magic of modern life with its mysteries and marvels. I was like a blind man suddenly able to see.

I was twenty-five years old, but my mind was no more sophisticated than that of a child, and I was bewildered and a little afraid of what I found. There I resolved to settle down and work, and there I also met the woman who would become my wife.

By coincidence, she arrived in Darjeeling one week after I did. Although I had met her many times in Khunde, I had never paid much attention to her, maybe because of the impoverished lives that both of us led there, and maybe also because of the monotony of our existence. But this time, when I saw her again in Darjeeling, something inexplicable drew us together, and soon we fell in love. She lived with her father and her older brothers. Fortunately they had a favorable opinion of our relationship. She was eighteen and I was twenty-five. She was born in Namche Bazaar and had spent her entire childhood in the Sherpa region, but her father often traveled to Tibet, sometimes with my father, even though our families barely knew each other.

I stayed in Darjeeling for nearly a year, much to my parents' chagrin. As is to be expected, they were worried at the thought of me leaving them. Their fears were logical. By that time I was very attached to my future in-laws, and I even traveled to Tibet with them.

With them, I left Darjeeling for Kalimpong. After stopping there for a few days, we kept going to Sikkim via Algarah and Rhenok, then to Kapup. I had to earn money for my trip by carrying, without an export license, a carton of cigarettes for a trader in Phari Dzong. This involved taking contraband goods from Sikkim to Tibet and required me to travel alone through the scrub. I had to split off from my companions who went ahead to Yatung. It was understood that I would rejoin them after completing my task. When I reached Yatung, I met up with a relative who worked as a courier, more specifically as a postal runner. We were overjoyed to see each other again, and he begged me to come to his house, which allowed me to stay in Yatung for as long as my future wife and her father had business to do there. Her father was collecting medicinal plants and herbs. This district is famous for them, and the traditional doctors in Kalimpong would buy them.

Yatung remains dear to my heart. My wife and I became engaged there, and we decided to marry as soon as possible. The five months of our engagement were among the happiest of our lives.

We were married when we returned to Darjeeling, and we settled there. Because my parents came up with a reason, my wife and I visited them in Khunde a few months later.

| 2 |

TRAVELS TO TIBET

WHEN WE TRAVELED TO TIBET, my father and I usually went to Kyetrak, a Tibetan village on the other side of the Nangpa La, about fifty kilometers from the border.[1] We walked together with about fifteen other people from Khunde and the surrounding villages.

Kyetrak is a major Tibetan trading center, and we had excellent relationships with the people who lived there. Marriages between residents of our two villages were common. We were always warmly welcomed in Kyetrak and stayed in friends' houses. We never stayed longer than two days and then returned home as soon as our business was finished.

During my first trip to Kyetrak with my father, we were crossing the Nangpa La when I developed a strange, splitting headache and had trouble seeing. My head was spinning and I felt vertigo coming on. I couldn't think clearly, and I lost track of where I was going. My eyes would not focus, and I had to lean on my father, who guided me over the pass. Even after we descended to a lower altitude, I collapsed several times, and my father was obviously still worried. But after we walked a few more kilometers, my eyesight and balance came back little by little. For the first time, I noticed the sparkling peaks around us. My friend Nim Tharkay pointed to the closest one and told me that it was called Sharmi Lo, and that, if I could throw a stone over it, I would be cured of all my aches and

pains. He explained that this mountain was sacred to the Sherpas and that the god who inhabited it wanted me to get his attention. The only way to do that was to throw a stone at him. Right then and there, I picked up a small rock and threw it at the huge white peak that looked sternly down at us from its great height. I was in such pain that I would have done anything, and I would have believed anything, no matter how crazy it sounded at the time. I didn't think about where my stone would land, and I didn't see that at best it would fall in the grass a few dozen meters away. Faith alone was my savior, and it seemed to me that my attempt had succeeded, because I immediately started to feel better.

The village of Chhule was our first stop. When we arrived, we found that a meal had been prepared for us. Everyone who traveled to Tibet by that route stopped for a day or two in this little village before continuing on. It was one of the few sections of the journey where the altitude was low enough for the weather to be reasonably warm. Chhule's soil was covered with fine, dry desert sand that was warmed by the sun. We all hurried to dive into it, roll in it, and rub our bodies and limbs with it to warm up and get our circulation flowing.

After we left Chhule, we headed next to Kungo Raba, where there was a hot spring lake. After our sand bath in Chhule, we would always go swimming there. We basked in the lake, and at that altitude the warmth was always shocking. Many people believe that that lake will cure any illness, and I'm sure that the water does have some healing powers.

Soon we came to the small village of Chipko, which held little interest for us. A little farther along, there was a steep slope of more than 300 meters, and we all prepared to climb it by rubbing our chests and breathing deeply. We climbed single file, joined by a rope tied around our waists. It was a brutal climb, and it took us nearly three hours to reach the small city of Lunak at the very top of the hill. Lunak is a major meeting place. It has a *dharamsala,* or rest house, that our people built especially for Sherpas traveling to Tibet, and we stopped there for the night. The dharamsala is a small, one-story building made of stone blocks, and it has a wooden roof covered with earth and thatch. It was extremely hard to find anything to

burn for fuel, and we had to gather and store any wood we could find so that we could burn it on our return trip. Otherwise, we were afraid that no one would have wood for us when we came back. We crisscrossed the forest to search for wood, and we even buried our food so that we wouldn't have to cook during our return trip.

After we left Lunak, the trip became very difficult. There were no places to stay, and it was almost impossible to find food. We had to make do with what we found along the trail, fruits and edible plants that nature offered us. The journey was so exhausting and we were so ravenous that we gnawed on everything we found, even tree roots and bark.

From Lunak, we headed to Ja Tsampa. There we were happy to see a little bit of sun after the difficult, grim, gray days we had just gone through. It shone brightly and warmed us up. We were now at an altitude of nearly 4800 meters, and we were approaching the snow-covered Nangpa La. This was the hardest section of the journey at 5800 meters. To cross it, we had to jettison all of our blankets, rugs, and other warm layers. When we reached the top of the pass, we saw nothing but a vast expanse of blinding white snow. During my first crossing, I had trouble knowing where to go. But my father and the other travelers were completely accustomed to walking over this pass in the snow.

It took us three days to cross the pass and reach Ja Po Wa on the other side. There we rested a bit before we continued on to Palung, a small city in Tibetan territory where we stopped in a dharamsala like the one in Lunak. But all of the travelers appreciated this one even more, as they were exhausted from crossing the pass, and some had gotten sick along the way.

The rest of the route to Palung is just a steady descent from the Nangpa La. The valley is magnificently green, and the forest is not so stifling. Waterfalls glisten on the banks of the steep cliffs, and ice gleams on the sheer walls above.

Palung is only about five kilometers from Kyetrak, and we covered that distance in less than an hour, although we usually stopped on a rocky outcrop where we could see the ruins of Dje Naza, an ancient Buddhist monastery one-and-a-half kilometers from Kyetrak.

We made this trip to Tibet nearly every year and sometimes more often. Our relationship with the Tibetans was one of brotherhood. They are the same ethnicity as we are, and several centuries ago we were also governed by Tibet. Many of our people settled in Tibet, and over the course of my several trips there, I went to visit many, many friends, and in their homes I always felt like family.

| 3 |

SHERPA COUNTRY AND
ITS INHABITANTS

As AN INTRODUCTION TO THIS chapter, I will cite a few lines from Eric Shipton's book *Mount Everest Reconnaissance Expedition, 1951*, in which the author says:

> *For twenty years, ever since I had first known the Sherpas, I longed, above all else, to visit their land of Sola Khumbu, through which the expedition would travel. I had heard so much about it from the Sherpas; indeed during our journeys together in other parts of the Himalaya and Central Asia, whenever we came upon a particularly attractive spot, they invariably said, "This is just like Sola Khumbu," and the comparison always led to a long, nostalgic discourse about their homeland. It required only an intelligent glance at the map and a little imagination to realize that their praise was not exaggerated; moreover, we had looked down into the upper valleys of Khumbu from the peaks west of Everest. Almost unknown to Western travelers, it had become, to me at least, a kind of Mecca, an ultimate goal in Himalayan exploration.*

Shipton is a very well known English writer, a learned and wise man, as well as the brave and competent leader of many Himalayan expeditions. I accompanied him beginning in the first years of my career as a Sherpa, and he taught me nearly everything that I needed to know about modern, scientific mountaineering, from how to study an itinerary and do reconnaissance to how to climb and set up high-altitude camps, and I am fiercely grateful to him for this. But in no way do I have all of his admirable qualities, and therefore I can only describe my small Himalayan homeland in the way that a humble, uneducated mountain man knows how to do.

Solu-Khumbu, "the country of the Eastern mountains," covers approximately 650,000 hectares and runs the entire length of the Dudh Kosi ("Milk River"), a tributary of the Sun Kosi ("Big River"). It is part of Nepal, one of the country's administrative districts. The region's major trading center is Namche Bazaar. Other large villages are Thame, Khumjung, Porchi, Pangboche, and Tengboche. Another village in Solu-Khumbu is Khunde, where I was born. Most of these villages are Buddhist religious centers, and there are monasteries where Nepali and Tibetan pilgrims often visit.

Our region is divided into two parts that are nearly equal in size: the northern part is called the Khumbu, and the southern part is called the Solu. More Sherpas live in the north part than in the south, where the ground is less fertile and there are thick forests nearly everywhere, if the ground is not completely covered with rocks.

There are no roads in the Khumbu. The only way to travel is by mountain paths, and the only methods of transportation are mules, Himalayan ponies, and the human back, as Sherpas are renowned worldwide as porters. A Sherpa's broad shoulders and solid kidneys make it possible to carry loads up to thirty-five or even forty kilos.

Nepal's capital, Kathmandu, is located approximately 160 kilometers to the west of Solu-Khumbu, and Darjeeling is 220 kilometers to the southeast. The Nangpa La, the pass on the Tibetan border, lies about 100 kilometers to the northwest.

Mount Everest rises just above our region, and Everest's little brother, Makalu, is a little farther away, maybe thirty kilometers to the northeast. The most beautiful view of the Everest massif is from the end of the long

Imja Khola valley, from Tengboche, Pangboche, and Porchi. So we are practically in the heart of the massif, where all of the peaks have Tibetan names that invoke life and power.

It rains more in the Solu than in the Khumbu, where the average yearly precipitation is never more than 1250 millimeters. Hailstorms are rare in the Khumbu but frequent in the Solu. In the Khumbu it snows a great deal, but rain is so rare that we sometimes have to melt snow to get water. I remember a year when the snowfall was so heavy that our houses were buried, and everyone in the village was imprisoned in their houses for a day.

Some rivers come down from the Chuttok La and the Kori La, which separate some villages in Sherpa country from an entirely different population: the Kirat tribe. Two rivers, the Thami Khola and the Imja Khola, form the borders of what we call Sherpa country.

As I mentioned, Namche Bazaar is the largest village in the Khumbu district. Here traders from Tibet and other regions in Nepal often gather to trade their wares. Everything that Sherpas might need, including food and clothes, they must go to Namche Bazaar to buy. We also go to Namche for festivals and melas [fairs]. It is the only place that we can find a little amusement in our isolated region, and it is the only place to meet up with strangers. So any self-respecting Sherpa, once he has the necessary time and money, must make a visit to Namche.

Namche Bazaar is at an altitude of 3720 meters. It is a group of seventy to eighty houses, and most of them are stone. They are all built in the same style, long and flat, but some have two stories and some have only one. They have between two and five rooms. One of the rooms, generally near the entryway, is used to house livestock, because they are an essential part of our property. Keeping livestock in the house is very common in Sherpa country.

The term "Sherpa" dates back to the time of Tibetan rule, years and years ago. In Tibetan it means "the Eastern people," from the words *sher*, meaning "East," and *pa*, meaning "people." All Sherpa names and our naming system come from Tibetan, and even our language is largely made up of Tibetan words. The residents of Solu are called Sore, and those who live between Solu and Khumbu, in the central region, are called Phar-ka-wa. Finally, the recent Tibetan immigrants who live in the Khumbu are called Khamba.

There are nineteen Sherpa clans: the Sherpa themselves (the primary clan), the Thakto, the Shire, the Sha-la-ka, the Chhu-Sherpa, the Pal-dorje, the Khamba-chen, the Men-de, the Lama-murmin, the Shyam-gup, the Pang-karma, the Kamba, the Phi-nasa, the Goley, the Go-farma, the Cha-ba, the Ghar-ja, the Yuk-pa, and the Gharti. The first five are the upper clans and the last five are the lower clans. The Gharti clan is considered the lowest of all.

Our religion is a form of Buddhism, which our ancestors adapted to our way of life. As mountain people, living right at the foot of the world's highest peaks, we have naturally been tempted to believe in the existence of mountain gods. Every village worships a specific divinity depending on which peak the village is closest to. We practice a type of Lamaism, but we also place a great deal of importance on sorcery and necromancy, and I believe that we are more intent on consulting shamans and following their instructions than on observing our lamas' or priests' dictates, to such an extent that our shamans have a much greater influence on our people than the true religious leaders do.

The shaman is called a *lhawa*. This is the person you go to see when you are sick, when something bad happens to you, or during a famine or a natural disaster. The lhawa usually knows the most important Buddhist writings and religious rites and serves as the guide for our consciences. In general we only go to see our true religious leaders, our lamas, to officiate at birth, marriage, and death ceremonies.

Some people in the village raise livestock and export most of their animals to Tibet. The slaughtered animals' hides are used to make dochas, Sherpa boots. Sherpas never slaughter their own animals. We hire Tibetan butchers, called *markes*.

Yak is a Sherpa's favorite meat. The animal's head and bones are put in clay pots where they are left to cure for two or three months, beginning in November or December. Once the meat and bones have marinated, we eat them during the summer. The other parts are cooked on the spot and are used to make soups and other dishes. Because we live in a cold climate, meat keeps for a long time. But most of my compatriots are too poor to allow themselves the luxury of eating meat. We also store carrots and turnips for

long periods of time in containers that we bury in deep pits. The vegetables are practically dried by the time we eat them.

Sherpas believe that no mules or horses should cross the Nangpa La, the highest pass in our area. It looms above us and is shaped like a horse's head. Because the mountain god has taken on the form of a horse, it is certainly forbidden to approach him with animals of the same species. So all Sherpas must climb the pass on foot.

The group of mountains that surround our district are known as the Five Sisters: Thamserku, Kangtega, Ama Dablam, Lhotse, and finally Everest itself, the oldest, which towers over all the others. There is another group farther to the northwest, with Lobuche (more often known as Pumori), Thobuche, and Cho Oyu.

Many different kinds of trees grow in our area, along with herbs and other plants that can be used for medicinal or other purposes. Among them are the *olere* (teak tree), the *salle*, the *dhupi*, the birch tree, the *charba*, the *langma*, and the *metang* (oil tree). We use sap from the metang for lamp oil, in place of kerosene or other oils that are difficult for us to obtain and too expensive for us to buy.

There are three kinds of grasses that are very precious to us: *richa*, which has thick, tender leaves; *chabu*, which is dense and straight; and *bawa*, which is a kind of tall lemongrass. In our valleys, we also have bamboo in abundance, particularly a variety that is especially thick and strong, which we call *malingo*. We generally store forage for our livestock in large barns over the winter. Our animals always have more than enough food, since our mountain slopes are always richly covered with grass.

Sherpas celebrate various festivals throughout the year. Groups of eight or ten families take turns making all of our annual preparations for Dumdze. This festival takes place in June or July, and these families must put on the celebration for the entire village. The members of those families meet on the first day of the festival, to make sure that everything has been done for the village to celebrate together. The second day is reserved for the lamas, and we offer a banquet for them. On the third day, we prepare *torma*, a home-brewed liquor, and in the evening we have a drinking contest. On the afternoon of the fourth day, the entire village gathers to eat a feast of rice

and heavily spiced meat. The feast lasts until midnight. The festival continues the next day when we drink chang. On the sixth day, there is a major religious ceremony at the monastery, where the lamas recite ritual prayers. On the seventh and final day, the festival ends with everyone dancing and the lamas singing as they collect contributions, which we call a *terma*, from everyone in the village for the upkeep of the monastery. Once the collection is done, the families in charge of the festival for the next year are selected from a list kept by the lamas, and each of them receives some of the terma.

The other festivals that we celebrate are Losar (the Tibetan New Year) and Yerdzang, the livestock festival that applies only to chauris, the offspring of yaks and Indian cows.

We celebrate Losar in the Tibetan way, with new clothes, exchanging compliments with our neighbors and friends, and feasting and drinking that lasts for a week. Yerdzang, celebrated annually in July by those who own chauris, is a bit more sedate and intimate than the other festivals. Families enjoy a rustic feast at home that includes a cake made out of *tsampa*, a type of kneaded flour dough made with ghee, clarified butter, and molded into the shape of the Himalayan mountains. After the religious ceremonies, prayers, and a banquet with drinking, the cake is cut and passed out to the guests.

Marriage among the Sherpas is a solemn occasion. The groom's male representatives visit the bride's home, bringing chang and *khatas*, or ceremonial scarves. They officially ask the young woman's parents or guardian for her hand in marriage. If the request is granted, the bride's parents and family offer a khata to every member of the groom's delegation, along with servings of a liqueur called *phemar*, which is very strong and quickly makes one drunk. Then it is the groom's turn to send the bride's family a dowry, either money or goods. After several months or more, the grooms' representatives return to the bride's house to decide on a date for the wedding. This visit is called the *pejang*, or "setting the date." On the day of the wedding, the groom goes to the bride's house dressed in a special outfit, and the ceremony takes place there. The future husband and wife sit next to each other and the lama anoints them with ghee on their heads, hands, and feet, and then makes a bright red mark on their foreheads. After joining their hands and saying a few prayers, the lama gives them a *yam-dam*, a swastika cross with

entwined spokes. Then he binds their hands together and implores them to behave as a faithful husband and wife. The ceremony ends with drinking, a banquet, and celebrations, and the young couple receives gifts such as livestock or clothing. The groom returns alone to his house until the next morning, when the bride arrives in a procession with her bridesmaids to take up residence in her new home.

When a child is born, a stranger may not visit the parents or eat in their home until the third day, when a lama performs a purification rite. The lama burns incense throughout the house, sprinkles holy water, and recites prayers as prescribed by the scriptures. A cake of rice and melted butter is then prepared and served to the people present, beginning with the lama. If the child is a boy, someone places a meter of white fabric, a *gotar* ("white scarf"), with a silver rupee sewn into one corner, in his hand for a minute or two. This is to remind him that he must support his family. Then the lama gives the child a name.

When a Sherpa dies, the body is cremated. The body is not taken from the house until three days after the death, and for three days lamps burn all day and all night around the body. The lama comes each day to recite the appropriate passages from the scriptures. On the fourth day, the body is placed on a litter and brought to the cremation location in a procession. Once the cremation is complete, the funeral guests each receive a *seer* of salt. For all of the next week, the lamas continue reading from the sacred texts, to pray for the dead person to rest in peace. On the seventh day, if the deceased is from a rich family, the last funeral ceremony is held: the entire village gathers after sunset for a festival that sometimes lasts long into the night. For the next three weeks, the villagers receive beer and rice, and at the end of the third week a final ritual meal is held. The entire village is invited, and everyone sings the praises of the deceased.

The Khumbu is administered by a village council elected by the people. Each village is represented by one member. The council members choose one member as president, to lead the Namche Bazaar council. All conflicts and questions are submitted to the council by the representative of the village in question. The council has complete power to make a decision, except in the case of a crime. Crimes are judged only by the district

court in Okhaldhunga. The village council is also responsible for collecting taxes and sending the money to the treasury department in Okhaldhunga. There is only one police station for all of Solu-Khumbu, located in Namche Bazaar, and there is no post office in the district. Mail is sent from village to village by "runners." Letters for outside the region are taken to the Okhaldhunga post office.

The central government has not built any major roads or public buildings in Solu-Khumbu. Only one of our roads is open all year. It begins in Okhaldhunga, runs near Taksindu and crosses the Dudh Kosi, and then heads toward Namche Bazaar. There is no industry in our area, which means that we have only our crops and our livestock to live on. To a lesser extent, we can work as porters during mountaineering season. And undoubtedly that is how we will have to live until the end of time.

Sherpas are born mountain climbers. Since the earliest explorations of Everest, Sherpas have been indispensable for every expedition. From one end of the Himalayan range to the other, all the way to the Karakoram at the northwest end, Sherpas have carried loads and set up camps for all of the expeditions and have served as staff for them. One might say it was Sherpas who made these expeditions possible.

Sherpas participated in the first assault on Everest by [George] Mallory, [Edward] Norton, [Howard] Somervell, and General C. G. Bruce in 1922. Seven Sherpas died on that attempt, which reached an altitude of 8200 meters, a magnificent accomplishment for that era of mountaineering. Then came the infamous Bruce and Mallory expedition of 1924, one of the noblest testaments to human will and bravery. On that expedition, well-known alpinists and some humble Sherpas sacrificed their lives for the cause. That was thirty years ago, and some twenty expeditions have taken place since. Sherpas were indispensable to all of them. In *Everest 1933*, Hugh Ruttledge wrote this story of an incident that is a good illustration of the Sherpa spirit:

> *The eastern slopes of the North Col are formed by what is, in fact, a steeply falling glacier. This presents the first serious obstacle. The*

place looks, from the east, like an almost vertical wall of snow and ice, some 1,200 feet high, seamed by crevasses and broken into great ice-cliffs. As the glacier is continually on the move, these features change from year to year, and each expedition has been obliged to choose its own route of ascent. Below, the East Rongbuk glacier runs first east, then north, then west, on its way towards the main Rongbuk glacier and the Base Camp.

Such was the mountain we were now to tackle. But illness was first to cause further delay. Ondi, one of our strongest porters, went down with double-pneumonia, a disease serious enough at all times, but terribly so at the altitude of the Base Camp, 16,800 feet. He was promptly put to bed in a Meade tent, given a continuous oxygen supply, and watched all night by climbers and porters. Greene and McLean soon decided that this was not enough, and that if his life were to be saved he must be carried down to a lower altitude, in the Kharta valley, five marches away. It was a last hope, for his condition was very serious. Poor Crawford, whose bronchitis also made a descent advisable, was detailed to take charge of a small body of Tibetan carriers. It was a bitter disappointment for him, but he rose to the occasion. Ondi was carried off one fine morning, giving a pathetic salute of the hand as he went, and McLean accompanied the party as far as Rongbuk.

The subsequent story of Ondi is worth recording, as an illustration of Sherpa spirit. When he left us, his life was despaired of. Just four weeks later, and against all orders, he turned up at the Base Camp, a heavy load on his back, and demanded work on the mountain. He is one of those rough characters, a sore trial to lovers of the quiet life, but a real thruster in time of storm and stress. Ondi is liable at any time to fall foul of the Darjeeling police. To us, he will always be the stout fellow who, scorning the ease of a convalescent camp, set an example of courage and devotion to duty. On the very day on which he collapsed he had carried a load to Camp I without complaint.

The incident reported by Ruttledge provides a characteristic example, from among hundreds of other examples that I could cite, of the Sherpa spirit and the Sherpas' deep love of the mountains. I know some Sherpas, many of whom are still alive today, who never missed a single expedition and who were always among the first to volunteer.

Nim Dorje's son, a "tiger" who died on the German expedition to Nanga Parbat in 1934, was only twenty years old and had already been on two expeditions.[2] He was particularly skilled in tracking Yeti, the "Abominable Snowman." Let us not forget that the Nanga Parbat expedition took the lives of seventeen of the twenty Sherpas who took part in it.[3]

Pemba Norbu, a veteran of the high mountains, only missed one expedition.[4] Although he is now more than fifty years old, we still see him scaling the snowy slopes of the high peaks. His son, Pasang Phutar, twenty-five, has already taken part in two expeditions: the Swiss expedition in 1952 and Sir John Hunt's historic expedition of 1953.[5]

Pasang Phutar lost two fingers on his right hand during the Godwin Austen (K2) expedition, and he was given a horse as compensation. During that same expedition, four other Sherpas died while trying to save one of the European climbers from the snow.[6]

During Mallory's attempt on Everest, six Sherpas died in an avalanche.[7] Three others died during the 1936 Nanda Devi expedition.[8] Ang Tsering, Da Tsering, Rinsing, Ching Tharkay, Kitar, Pasang Kikuli, and Nima Thunda also died on other expeditions, victims of the call of the mountains.[9]

The oldest living Sherpa is named Thami. He is over sixty and lives in Darjeeling. Other veterans also live in Darjeeling, such as Ang Temba, fifty-eight; Bonu, fifty-six; and the sirdar Hishe, who will soon turn sixty.[10]

Sherpanis, or Sherpa women, also offer their services to climbing expeditions. They are called on to work at base camps and up to altitudes of 6300 meters. Many of them accompany their husbands or brothers and are just as passionate about mountain climbing as the men are.

The youngest qualified Sherpa I know is Ang Chering. Since the age of eighteen he has been climbing to an altitude of 6600 meters, and he would have gone higher if he had been allowed to. He was part of the Hunt team

in 1953. He is a young man with a bright future, and he hopes to someday find himself among the champions.

I don't want to conclude this chapter without a heartfelt mention of a dear friend, who came from a neighboring village in the Khumbu. His name was Jigme Sherpa, and we participated in many expeditions.[11] We were about the same age. He had been hired by the German expedition to Nanga Parbat, while I was hired by Shipton's Karakoram group. We spent our last night in Srinagar, in Kashmir, together. We had stopped there for three days before meeting up with our respective employers. When it came time to part, it seemed to me that Jigme had a premonition that we would never see each other again, and he gave me his wristwatch to remember him by. Our goodbyes were full of sadness, and then we parted. Alas! His premonition was not wrong, and when I came back from the Karakoram six months later, I found out in Gilgit about the Nanga Parbat disaster.[12] For me, the news was terrible, and I couldn't hold back my tears: it felt as if I had lost a beloved brother. I kept his watch as a testament to our friendship. When I returned, I burned lamps and incense in his memory at the large Rongbuk Monastery. Unfortunately his watch, which I kept as a precious relic, was lost along with all of my belongings in Chomo Yomo, in southern Sikkim, during a reconnaissance mission that I did there with Mr. Tully.[13]

| 4 |

I Choose a Career as a Sherpa

I CANNOT REALLY SAY WHAT drew me to the whirlwind of high mountain expeditions. As a child, isolated in the village where I was born and completely unaware of the outside world, I barely knew what mountain climbing was.

I was a little older than twenty when I met Nim Tharkay, one of my friends from the village, who was returning from General Bruce's expedition. He was coming to see me at home in Khunde, still carrying all of his climbing equipment. He strutted from house to house as if he had just accomplished something awe-inspiring. As I was younger than he was, my imagination ran wild when I heard his sensational descriptions of his adventures. I was so impressed that I immediately felt an uncontrollable desire to follow his example and try to join an expedition myself. I did not leave his side and listened avidly as he told of his adventures in the mountains.

Shortly thereafter, I went with Nim Tharkay to Oaku, a Rai village fairly far from Khunde, to get the grain provisions that both of our families needed. The journey took us about three days, so we had time to talk and, of course, our only topic of conversation was Nim Tharkay's climbs and adventures. My enthusiasm and interest grew. I could think and talk of nothing else. Perhaps destiny hopped on board with my desire. Along the way, we had stopped at the home of a Sherpani who had just come back from Darjeeling.

She told us that a new expedition was underway, and that they were hiring young Sherpas. She told us that the sirdar Gyalgen still had several spots available on his team, and she enthusiastically encouraged me to go there and apply.[1] She was a young woman, about my own age, who was also enthusiastic about these adventures, and she made me wish I were in Darjeeling just then.

We went home the next day with our provisions. Along the way, I met up with another of my friends, Jigme Sherpa, who would meet his death on Nanga Parbat soon after. As he also had some climbing experience, I went to ask his advice. I told him about the news that the woman had shared with me, and about my intense desire to go immediately to Darjeeling and apply for a job. He told me that it was not complicated. I didn't need to take anything with me, because the organizers would provide me with everything I needed: clothing, blankets, mountain climbing shoes, et cetera. I only needed a small amount of money to pay for my expenses on the way to Darjeeling. Jigme was so happy about my enthusiasm that he offered his wool coat to me to sell in order to raise the money that I needed. The next morning, I went to Namche Bazaar with my father. Once we had done our shopping, my father decided to return home that same evening. I told him that the *makai* (corn) that we had purchased needed to be ground into flour, and I asked him to leave me in Namche to take care of it. He agreed and went home alone. During my stay in Namche, I went to the bazaar to listen to people talking about the new expedition that was being organized. I asked them questions, and they told me that the expedition would not leave until at least a week later. I was happy to learn that I still had time to ask for a job, so I returned to Khunde with the flour, and then I left for the Khari-Khola without attracting any attention. This journey normally takes three days, but I was so nervous and excited about my adventure that I walked quickly and reached Oaku two mornings later. There I went to see a friend who very kindly invited me to have dinner and stay with him for several days, but I declined his offer because I was in such a rush to find Jigme Sherpa. I couldn't locate him that night, but I found Ang Pasang instead.[2] He was preparing to return to his village, and I was unsuccessful in convincing him to accompany me to Darjeeling.

I left Oaku at night, for fear that the Kirat people would tell my father about my disappearance. I slipped stealthily out of my host's house and found Jigme, who was waiting for me one hundred meters away. Together we headed for Darjeeling. We walked all night and reached Solang the next morning. We did not have any money to speak of, but we met a friend of Jigme's in a teahouse, and he gave us a snack. After a brief rest in Solang, we continued our journey. We crossed the Solba ridge and reached Tumlingtar after crossing the Arun River on a raft. With my last Nepali rupee, I paid the six annas that the river crossing cost for the two of us.

Tumlingtar is famous for its rustic pottery, made from a local variety of clay. We purchased two pots in which to cook our meals. Jigme had brought corn flour with him, and fortunately that would be enough for us on our journey. We drank a glassful of local chang and continued on our way. We were not at all bothered by the prospect of making the entire journey on foot, because we wanted badly to reach Darjeeling before it was too late. So we walked fairly quickly despite our empty stomachs and the steep, seem-ingly endless trail. We went through Terhathum, a Limbu village, and just past Terhathum is the Tamur River. I had assumed that we would cross the river on foot, but Jigme warned me not to count on that: it was dangerous, full of treacherous pools. As with the Arun, we would have to cross on a raft. After that, we reached the village of Panthar, in the heart of Limbu coun-try. When we arrived, a local person was being cremated, and the funeral ceremony was taking place on top of a hill. The funeral was accompanied by a feast of roasted meat and chang, and all of the guests were invited. We were greatly relieved to take advantage of the occasion, because we were very hungry and completely out of money. While we were gorging ourselves, a village elder advised us to leave as soon as possible, because the Lim-bus would soon be drunk, and, when night fell, any stranger in the village might find himself under attack. We headed for Singalapa, bringing with us enough chang for the journey.

On the trail between Singalapa and Ilam, two men who we knew joined us. They were also going to Darjeeling, so now we formed a small troop. Toward evening, we reached Simina, where we camped in an empty shack. There we were able to grind our corn and collect some wood to build a fire.

We left Simina the next morning and finally arrived at Darjeeling at the stroke of eleven o'clock. Our two companions left us there.

We wandered around Chowk Bazaar, with the hope of meeting some people we knew. We had the good fortune of running into our old friend Mingma Thu Thu, who has since accompanied Tilman on his expedition to Rakaposhi.[3] We asked him to find lodging for us. He told us that my aunt's daughter now lived in Darjeeling, and she had just returned from a stay in Benares. This was good news for us, and we hurried on our way to her home. She welcomed us most cordially and offered us her hospitality. Next, we rushed to the Himalayan Club's hiring office.

Unfortunately, the new expedition had already departed, and we had arrived too late. But we had to find work. At that time, the Victoria Hospital was being built, and I got a job there as a laborer—my job was to carry rocks. After three months, I was hired by one Nima Tempa to transport goods to Pemionche. We formed caravans of twelve Sherpas and carried the goods on our backs. We were each paid an advance of three rupees, which was not enough to cover our expenses along the way. We had to pool our money and buy, ahead of time, all of the provisions that we might need on the trail. It took ten days to reach Pemionche, and we found ourselves with no more resources and with too little money to return to Darjeeling. Nima Tempa abandoned us to our own devices, despite the fact that we were almost dead from hunger and fatigue.

For better or worse we returned to Darjeeling, and my friend Mingma Thu Thu suggested that I go and register with Gyalgen, who was in charge of hiring staff for expeditions. I did so as soon as possible. But a man named Tobi was also in charge of hiring, and I did not know that he had previously been Gyalgen's business partner. There had been a conflict of interest, and the two had had a falling out. Tobi had arranged to keep most of the business for himself, leaving only a small clientele for Gyalgen.

I arranged to win Tobi's trust through a ruse that you might find unscrupulous. Everyone who had been hired by Tobi had received a brass badge to show that they were part of the staff for an expedition. I bought one of these badges from a Sherpa for five rupees, and I shamelessly impersonated him when I

went to see Tobi. He hired me immediately for the 1931 German expedition to Kanchenjunga. That was how I got started as an expedition Sherpa.

Base camp was set up near Green Lake on Zemu Glacier. We were promised that the first to arrive at the glacier would definitely be hired. Ang Song, three other Sherpas, and I were the first to arrive, but unfortunately, despite that, we were not hired. There were rivalries among the sirdars. They never kept their promises and selected their own protégés. For us this was a bitter disappointment, and we returned to Darjeeling dejected and deeply discouraged. I told Tobi about the incident, but he could not do anything, and so I was unemployed for June, July, and August, and I stayed with a relative in Darjeeling. Then Tobi asked me to go with him for some climbing practice in Selu-La-Tu. That was my first experience with the brutal and dangerous life of a climber. During the return trip, in Ching-Thung, I came down with jaundice. There were three of us with the same illness, and Tobi loaned us a horse. We took turns riding until we got to Gangtok. We were put to bed in the bungalow, the *daks* (travelers) house, and when Tobi arrived soon after, he found me nearly in a coma. He wanted to take me to the hospital immediately. I was very afraid, because I did not know what a hospital was. I thought that people were sent there to die. So I refused to go, and Tobi was very upset. He decided to leave me, come what may, and he continued on with the rest of the group. I was furious at being abandoned, and I tried in vain to follow him. Weak and sick, I had a great deal of trouble even standing up. I resolved to reach Singtam, which was a good distance from Gangtok, no matter what effort was required. I arrived there in four hours and rested at an inn in the village, where I drank a pot of chang. I felt horribly sick, and I had a nosebleed. I began to wonder if I would ever make it back to Darjeeling. I stayed in Singtam for four days and ate almost nothing. I had nothing to protect myself from the cold, and I had nearly no shelter against the wind that blew at night. I truly thought that my last hour on Earth had arrived, and I wondered what people would say at home. But undoubtedly the hour of our death is already determined, because at the end of the fifth day I felt a little better. I stumbled and limped for day upon day, fueled by the desire not to be on the trail any more. And with God's help,

after once again crossing the Tista River, I arrived back in Darjeeling after six weeks of superhuman effort.

When I arrived in Tumsang, on the outskirts of Darjeeling, I collapsed on the trail and was helped to my feet by a passerby who took me to the hospital. I was treated there for several days, and they sent for my brother-in-law. He immediately took me to his home, where I still had attacks of jaundice. My aunt was still staying with him as well. I honestly believe that without their care I would not be here today.

Three weeks later, my brother-in-law left on a journey, but my aunt delayed her departure for four months in order to take care of me. Before she left, she gave me a small amount of money to take care of my needs for a little while. The months passed, and one day I ran into a distant relative who advised me to go to Yatung to gather some medicinal plants and then sell them in Kalimpong. In the meantime, I had spent all of my money, and I had to pay for my trip to Yatung by carrying a load of cigarettes to Phari. For that I was paid five rupees. Flush with this money, I went to Yatung, where I met up with a few friends. I went with them to hunt for the medicinal plants that we could sell. We succeeded in picking nearly two mounds (seventy kilos) that we brought to Kalimpong. For this load we were paid twelve rupees. One month later, we were once again out of money, and I could not find any work. After being unemployed for some time and relapsing—my health was still not outstanding—I decided to return to Darjeeling and try my luck with an expedition once again.

A few days after I arrived, I was still feeling weak, and death still crossed my mind. I ran into Mingma Thu Thu who told me to go immediately to the Himalayan Club, where a new expedition was forming and Sherpas were being hired. I rushed there, saying a prayer that I would finally be granted the chance to seize the opportunity. When I arrived at the hiring office, I saw a crowd of Sherpas who were waiting to have their credentials reviewed. I got in line, but I was able to cut ahead a bit, and I was no more than twenty meters from the front of the line. I had no real hope of being hired, though, because I was feeling weak. My eyes were sunken and I was thin. My legs trembled underneath me.

I knew how slim my chances were, and when it was my turn, I proceeded humbly before the examiner. I answered the questions that I was asked, with a confidence and vigor that surprised me. I undoubtedly made a strong impression on the group that was responsible for selecting people, because, to my great joy, I was finally approved and sent to Victoria Hospital for a medical examination. There again providence protected me, because I was declared fit for service in the mountains. That is how I was hired for the 1933 Everest expedition organized by Hugh Ruttledge, who was planning to attack the mountain from the Tibetan side.

We left Darjeeling on March 3, 1933. It was a memorable date, one that will be forever etched in my memory as a Sherpa. The expedition's members were all British, under Mr. Ruttledge's direction. We were divided into three groups, and I was part of the first group to leave Darjeeling, via Kalimpong and Pedong. We then crossed Sikkim and continued on to Gautsa after crossing the 3600-meter Jelep-La.[4] We were now in Bhutan. From there the various groups in our expedition came together and embarked on the assault of the world's highest mountain. That is how I was introduced to the passion of Himalayan mountain climbing.

| 5 |

My Expeditions to Everest

I HAVE PARTICIPATED IN EIGHT expeditions to Everest.[1] Four have been from the Tibetan side. The goal of the most recent expedition was not so much to reach the summit as to prepare routes for a future conquest of the mountain. That reconnaissance expedition, which Eric Shipton undertook in 1951, undoubtedly had a decisive effect on Edmund Hillary and Tenzing Norgay's triumphant climb on Everest in 1953.

I am very grateful to Shipton for agreeing to make me a central part of his admirable exploration: looking for an access route that enabled the grand result that was achieved two years later. I am absolutely sure that without the 1951 expedition, Everest would not have been conquered in 1953, but the final assault was nonetheless a splendid achievement in its own right.

FIRST EXPEDITION (1933)

I WILL NOW RESUME MY story in chronological order and come back to my first Everest expedition, with Hugh Ruttledge, in 1933. Mr. Shipton was on this expedition as well.

We had stopped in Gautsa, planning to stay about one week to wait for the rest of the group who had left later than we did.[2] At the time, I was only a novice porter, and the older porters bullied me quite a bit, especially a certain Karma Paul, who constantly mocked

me despite my poor state of health, my weakness, and my inexperience. He made my life miserable. I had a horrible case of the flu and bronchitis, along with a high fever. We arrived in Shabre Subra in the middle of a snowstorm, and I was on the verge of collapse. I even thought that I would have to turn back, with Karma Paul ceaselessly telling me that I was good for nothing. In the afternoon we reached Khamba Dzong, where we were ordered to make camp. I had been assigned to the team that was responsible for setting up the tents for each bivouac, and this required me to work like a beast. We were only paid twelve annas per day, plus six annas as a food allowance.

Wangdi Norbu directed our team and made us work like slaves. This was more or less manageable during the day, but at night a violent, icy wind came up, and it was very hard to keep the tents standing for long. We stopped for a few days, then went on to Tengkey Dzong. It was a marvelous place, with large ponds covered with white ducks. We gained more and more altitude, and this first glimpse of the high mountains made me see life from a completely different perspective. I felt as if I had reached the top of the world, which enchanted me in a completely different way than the hill country that I came from. Most of my comrades were mountain veterans and naturally did not share my enthusiasm. My pain and weakness had disappeared, and I felt like a new man, completely ready to keep climbing forever.

We relaxed by playing various sports and games or rubbing ourselves with fresh snow. It was a very beautiful spot, and I was awash in happiness. After three days we left Tengkey Dzong and walked to Rongbuk, a fairly important Tibetan place. We paid a visit to the lamas at the monastery, and they gave us their blessing. If we accomplished our task honestly, faithfully, and joyfully, they assured us that nothing bad could happen to us.

After two days we left Rongbuk. We went twenty-five or thirty kilometers farther to set up our base camp, then we sent the mules back down. The actual climb was now beginning, and it was up to us to carry the loads. We were very short on wood for heating, and we had to collect all of the brush that we could find along the route. More than once we were driven mad with hunger, with absolutely nothing to put in our mouths. We walked as fast as our legs could carry us, because we were in such a hurry to get to camp as fast as possible to prepare food.

Our base camp had been set up in a place called Chi-Long-Mamo, which in Tibetan means "home of the god Chi-Long." A solitary lama had built himself a hermitage out of a cave chiseled into a rock surrounded by grass. It was an unexpected sight at these desert-like altitudes. We didn't fail to visit the lama. At that time he was about thirty years old and seemed completely normal and in good health. He gave us his blessing and told us that he would pray for us.

Life in base camp held no real appeal for us Sherpas. The expedition organizers barely treated us as humans. The latrines that had been built were reserved exclusively for the "sahibs." We had to relieve ourselves some distance away. In the dark, some of us accidentally wandered into the forbidden area. We were severely punished, and Karma Paul, who had us under his direct orders, exercised his prerogatives with absolutely no restraint, forcing each of us to pay a fine of eight annas.

We were intensely dissatisfied, because we were barely paid enough to eat, and we were ravenously hungry. But our anger evaporated when we received the order to prepare for the actual climb.

We set off for Camp I a bit after mid-April, and we arrived on the twentieth. Camp I was located in a magnificent spot near the Rongbuk Glacier, from which we could see the sharp white peak of Pumori. After we set up camp, we continued on to Camp II, which was at an altitude of approximately 6000 meters, on the other side of the Rongbuk Glacier. A few Tibetan porters had joined us, but they could not keep up with us, and we left them along the way. While climbing from one camp to the next, I was always with the lead group, and because we were walking through the snow, I began suffering intensely from the cold. I sometimes had a very hard time catching my breath, because I was not yet acclimated to those altitudes. But I was absolutely determined to acclimatize myself and not to be left behind even once, although I was exhausted from fatigue.

We were provided with crampons so that we could walk on the ice. Camp III, at an altitude of 6400 meters, had to serve as a sort of intermediate base camp. The snow grew deeper. A layer of ice on top of the snow made walking difficult and dangerous, especially for me, because I was not accustomed to it. Also, we had to cut steps. It was not easy to chop away at the ice, and

more than one of us fell and was gravely injured. We had to climb steep, slick slopes, and the high winds made our work even more treacherous.

It was difficult for us to urinate into the wind. We had to stash empty food cans inside our clothes to be able to relieve ourselves. Because of this, empty cans were in high demand when we left camp, especially for the Tibetan porters, who were the most avid collectors of them. Above the intermediate camp, between Camps III and IV, we started having to use rope ladders. I had never used a rope ladder before, and I was a little nervous. But I quickly got used to it, and I was soon fairly skilled at this exercise.

I stayed at Camp IV until the next camp had been established.[3] That was done in two stages, with a bivouac in the middle. We could see Everest's breathtaking summit towering some 1800 meters above and directly across from us. My heart immediately began to pound, I was so moved by this sight. A bitter wind swirled mercilessly above us, blowing sheets of snow and ice that fell like rain around us. We had reached the critical point in the climb. We had to put forth a superhuman effort to establish Camp V, at an altitude of 7830 meters.[4]

Finally the assault team managed to create a route and set up the camp, despite immense difficulties. We arrived a little later. The wind was absolutely unbearable, and we Sherpas were almost paralyzed. Our tents were ripped out of the ice. Men were lifted off their feet and toppled against each other. Many of us were seriously injured and some thought that they would never get up again. The sahibs were very good to us. They made bandages for us and gave us food. The howling winds became more and more violent, and blocks of hardened snow fell around us like meteors. We worked for three days at Camp V, and then we were ordered to descend to Camp IV. On the descent, I found Pasang lying by the side of the trail, with almost no strength left. I lifted him up and nearly carried him to Camp IV.

When we arrived back at Camp IV, most of us were suffering from frostbite. I could no longer feel my hands or my feet, and I could neither rub them together nor use them. Kipa Lama made me some food and laid me down so that I could sleep. The Sherpas who were in the worst shape were taken down to Camp III, but I forced myself to stay strong. A new team of porters was formed to replace those who could not work, and

we set up Camp IV, which would serve as a base for the final assault. We finished our work in the evening, and at dusk we slipped into our tents to rest for a bit. The last rays of sunshine were shining brightly through the clouds, but the clouds grew darker in a worrisome way. Suddenly the air around us exploded with a violent clap of thunder and strange cries that sounded as if they came from an army of starving jackals. To this day we do not know what caused this.

The next morning [May 28, 1933], we climbed back to Camp V. Mr. Birnie made us tea, and the entire team—Mr. [E. St. J.] Birnie, Mr. [Wyn] Harris, Mr. [Laurence Rickard] Wager, Mr. [John Laurence] Longland, and the Sherpas Da Tsering, Ang Tsering, Rinsing Bhotia, Pasang Bhotia, Tsering Tharkay, Kipa Lama, Nim Dorje, and myself—pushed ahead to establish Camp VI.[5] We reached the spot in the evening. It was a sinister place, glacial and desolate. It was a narrow cornice dominated by a large, rocky ridge. There was just barely room for three or four men. I wondered why the sahibs had chosen such a place, but what did I know about mountain climbing? After inspecting the spot, Mr. Longland took us back down to Camp IV, leaving only Mr. Harris and Mr. Wager at Camp V. We were cordially welcomed back at Camp IV, and the sahibs enthusiastically shook hands with us, congratulating us on our climb to Camp VI. After we were given a good amount of food, we were encouraged to descend to Camp III.

Along the way, I was greatly delighted to find, at the intermediate camp, a package and a letter "from my wife." The package contained fifty packs of cigarettes and a dozen boxes of matches. I had someone read the letter to me, since I could not read it myself. The friend who read it seemed to hesitate to tell me what it said, which made me worry that it contained bad news. But because I insisted, Kipa Lama took me aside and explained it to me. The letter was actually anonymous, meant only to disturb my serenity. For a reason of which I am unaware, the writer was jealous of me. I had absolute faith in my wife, and I loved her very much. And that filthy letter informed me that my wife had been unfaithful to me, that she had run off with another man, and that I had lost her.

Although that news was clearly untrue, it ate away at me to the point that I was constantly tortured by it. Mr. Ruttledge saw how much I was

worried and irritated, and he advised me to go back down to base camp to rest and get my mind straight. But I decided to return to Rongbuk to consult the lamas at the monastery, so that they would deliver me from this terrible lot that had been cast, and deflect my enemies' evil intentions and thus remove me from this humiliation.

After the lamas had blessed me, they comforted me and told me to have faith in God and to continue my work calmly and with confidence. I spent about two weeks in Rongbuk, and then I went back to camp. I felt relieved and once again in control of myself.

But although my mind was freer, my frostbitten fingers still had no feeling, as if they were dead. This caused me a great deal of suffering. The expedition doctor told me to bring back my circulation by cutting and gathering wood in the countryside, and by using my hands and legs as much as possible. We Sherpas did not understand the rationale for this treatment, and we wanted nothing to do with it. We had the impression that it was a way of taking advantage of us during the remainder of the vacation period that Mr. Ruttledge had granted us. We were all fined five rupees for disobedience, to be deducted from what we would be paid at the end of the expedition.

There were three attempts to progress beyond Camp VI, but all three had to be abandoned. When I returned from Rongbuk, I was sent to base camp to wait for new orders. My frostbite was not yet healed, and it caused me a great deal of pain and annoyance. A friend suggested cauterizing the wounds with red iron—a common treatment used by Sherpas—and I did. I discovered with surprise that I felt some relief from it. The doctor examined me and sent me back to Tashi Dzong with nine comrades. The sirdar Leba, who was one of our supervisors, had told me that I would come back to camp later for another attempt. For that reason he ordered me to leave all of my equipment in camp, including my ice axe. I was only allowed to take a thin wool blanket, and with that I left for Tashi Dzong. We stayed there for one month and then returned to base camp.

Along the way, shortly before arriving in Camp 1, I ran into my father through a sheer, lucky coincidence. I was very happy to see him again. He had not seen me since my wedding in Darjeeling, and he really did not know my wife at all. He was inclined to believe the rumors about her, and

he could not console me in any way about that situation. On the contrary, he advised me to go back home to the Khumbu and marry another woman. I was crushed and thoroughly discouraged. I had the feeling that I was being played, and I was consumed by anxiety about what was happening at my home in Darjeeling. I felt that all of the effort that I had put into succeeding as a professional Sherpa would be utterly meaningless in the face of my marital woes. But my ambition to successfully complete my apprenticeship despite and in the face of everything would be rewarded in the end, when I was selected from among all of my comrades to rejoin the expedition at its highest point.[6]

Once the decision had been made to abandon any more attempts on the summit, we received the order to pack up our things and return home. We left for Gangtok in June. We were paid six annas per day for expenses along the way from Gangtok to Darjeeling. As always, that was not enough to pay for our individual expenses, so we pooled our salaries, and that was just enough to feed us along the way. I thought only of my wife and my home in Darjeeling, and my mind swirled with evil thoughts. Most of my companions, on the contrary, were thoroughly happy to be returning home, and they brought souvenirs and knick-knacks from Tibet for their families.

I came back empty-handed and feeling as if my soul had died. When I arrived home, I discovered to my great joy that all was well, and that my wife, who was expecting our first child, was in perfect health and thrilled to see me. I was sorry that I had nothing to give her except my true and faithful love.

Here I will take the liberty of quoting a sentence, just a few words from Hugh Ruttledge's book *Everest 1933*: "Only one, the great-hearted little Ang Tarke, ever went high again." This humble sentence was worth volumes to me, because it was only my first attempt in the high mountains.

SECOND EXPEDITION (1935)

IN 1935, NEARLY TWO YEARS after my first expedition, I returned home after having worked as a guide for an American tourist. When I arrived in Diksha, I learned that Eric Shipton was en route with a new expedition. On the spot, I was seized with an intense desire to find him, because on the

Ruttledge expedition in 1933 he had been my leader, and in 1934 I had gone with him to Nanda Devi (see Part 2, Chapter 1). I left Diksha immediately with a comrade, heading to Darjeeling by the shortest and fastest route, in the hope of arriving in time to be hired. We reached Darjeeling in record time, three days, and had barely arrived when we learned that the hiring was done and that the first half of the expedition had already left. But, incredibly, Mr. Shipton was still there, and we hurried to the Himalayan Club to find him. He was shocked and thrilled to see us and hired us on the spot.

I took a day off to go see my family before leaving. The next day, fifteen of us reported for duty: seven Tibetans and eight Sherpas, including Tenzing Norgay, who was just starting out in mountaineering at that time.[7] We had been provided with a double (two-person) sleeping bag, and I was meant to share it with Tenzing. He told me to keep it at the end of this memorable expedition. To this day, I have kept this sleeping bag as a souvenir of Tenzing.

We were each ordered to carry a load of seventy pounds (approximately thirty-two kilos) from Gangtok to Lachen. As Sherpas were theoretically not required to serve as porters until after reaching base camp, we protested. We unanimously decided to strike and go home. Having made that decision in Lachen, we refused to go any farther on the central Tibetan plateaus with our loads.

The next morning, we packed our things and went as a group to the sahibs, asking that we be sent back. Mr. Shipton invited me in to talk. He tried to persuade me not to leave. I told him that I could do nothing to go against my comrades' decision. I felt that it was perfectly justified. What we were being required to do had never been done, and we considered it a breach of contract. Mr. Shipton was strongly in favor of resolving this dispute amicably. He asked us to agree to carry the loads for just one day, and, after that, other arrangements would be made. We agreed, and when we arrived in Thanggu the next day, a mule train was organized to free us from our loads.

We took a shortcut to reach the Gompa Lhabu pass via Thang Lung and Muk, and then we reached Sar, where we stopped for eighteen days. The sahibs explored the area while we helped out with work in camp.

Our Tibetan comrades took us to their homes, where we slept during the entire stay in Sar. During that break, there was an incident that gave a glimpse of real life in a Tibetan village. I imagine that this could happen in any other village as well. Tenzing and I had gone to a bar and ordered some chang. All of our Sherpa friends were there as well. A young Tibetan woman was the server, and she was very sweetly joking around with us. A young buck, the village leader's son, objected to our conversations with the young woman. In vulgar terms, he accused us of having dishonest intentions. My comrades, including Tenzing, immediately left without saying anything, leaving me alone to respond to these accusations. I walked up to the young man and asked him what he was trying to prove, insulting us with no rhyme or reason. I assured him that Sherpas are not libertines and that our conversation with the young woman was perfectly innocent. But he kept spewing insults, and I was seized with a fit of anger and punched him straight in the face. This caused such a ruckus that the boy's father soon arrived and asked me to punch him in the face instead of his only son. I did not know what to say, so I left, feeling very sheepish and ashamed.

The next day, the Tibetan father went to see Mr. Shipton and presented him with a khata, a scarf made of many pieces of fabric in different colors—it was a sign of politeness. Mr. Shipton then sent for me. I asked my comrades to come with me because the situation involved us all, but they ignored me, and I went alone. I saw the father, the mother, and the young man standing before Mr. Shipton and Karma Paul, and all of them glared at me. I immediately felt that I was not going to escape a severe punishment. Karma Paul ordered me to drape a khata around the father's neck as a sign of apology, and he ordered me to pay the father five rupees. I vehemently protested such an unfair decision. I had neither a khata nor any money with me. How was I supposed to do this when we were only paid six annas per day? I answered that I would go to Gyantsé or Shigatsé, where there was a Gurkha representative who would issue a fair judgment on the case. Mr. Shipton explained to me that because we were in Tibetan territory but did not yet have official authorization from the Tibetan government, this incident could have serious consequences, and it might compromise the success of our entire expedition. He gave me a khata so that I could offer it to the

Tibetan man. I gave it to him along with one rupee as a peace gesture. That ended the incident. My comrades said that they were satisfied, and they were grateful to me for taking responsibility for the incident without blaming them. They took up a collection to pay me back.

We left Sar for Rongbuk, a journey of seven days. We had to do a reconnaissance of the entire region from the north col of Kanchenjunga to the Kharta valley. Along the way, we set up Camps I, II, and III, and we stopped for an entire day at Camp III. The next day we kept walking, and along the trail, about 300 meters higher, we came upon the corpse of a European. The body was not decomposed, and the part that stuck out above the ground was shriveled and hairless. The lower portion of the body was buried and in perfect condition. The man had lost a shoe, and it looked as if he were trying to lace his other shoe with his hand. His eyes were closed. Rinjin, the Tibetan porter who had accompanied the sahib before his death, told us the story of what had happened. It was believed that he had come via Sikkim, and he was dressed in Tibetan clothing and appeared to have no passport. He must have changed into his mountaineering clothes after crossing the Tibetan border. Our expedition doctor examined him and could not say whether he had died of an illness or an injury.

Rinjin told us that he had walked with the sahib to Rainplu. After that, the sahib continued on alone, on the route by which he would never return. In his jacket pocket we found a date book in which there was a note with Rinjin's name, along with Tsering Tharkay's and Tewang Bhotia's.[8] Tsering and Tewang were also Tibetan and had been on our expedition in 1933, but they were not with us now. We carried the body away and buried it in a crevasse.

Before continuing on, it was decided that we should do a meticulous reconnaissance of the North Col. Mr. Shipton wrote about this in his book *Upon That Mountain*. He said that the body we found was that of Maurice Wilson, who had wanted to attempt a solo climb of Everest but died along the way.

Mr. Shipton stated that our expedition's goal was, above all, to prepare the team and study the terrain, ahead of an expedition that would take place during the next year, 1936. I had the impression that the sahibs saw

our expedition as a giant high-altitude picnic, because in addition to the enormous number of books that they had brought along, they had a sizable reserve stock of provisions, discovered in what we called the "Wilson hide-away." We also spent a good portion of our time collecting hundreds of eggs and whatever vegetables we could find in the surrounding villages.

The reconnaissance that the sahibs did on the North Col took a fairly long time. We Sherpas had almost no climbing to do beyond Camp III. We had almost no responsibilities other than helping the sahibs carry their instruments, provisions, and cookware. Our exploration area was around the Rongbuk Glacier and the Kharta valley, at altitudes that were rarely over 7000 meters.[9]

The expedition's work was done around the middle of July, and we began our return journey in the Kharta valley, passing near the high Arun valley—the Gatung Paga—that we had to cross on a rope bridge under extremely difficult and dangerous conditions. There was no other way to cross, and we all had to take the risk. Then the Sherpas who were returning to the Solu-Khumbu left us. The rest stopped on the steep slope with the sahibs, drinking *juar* (Tibetan wine) and taking a pleasant and relaxing break before continuing the journey.

We rested there for forty-eight hours while the sahibs did a reconnais-sance in the surrounding hills, then we left for Thanggu via Lunak. In Thanggu the sahibs gave us a tent as a gift to thank us for our good service. We could not all use it together, so we ripped it into pieces that we dis-tributed among ourselves. When we arrived in Chang-Thang, there were no longer enough in our team, so we hired two coolies to carry the expe-dition's instruments and papers. The new porters could not keep up with us, and we arrived in Singlik long before them. This made Mr. Shipton very angry. He was outraged because we had abandoned the expedition's important instruments and papers. He ordered us to walk to Gangtok as fast as possible. We could not blame him, because we were also worried about the coolies who were late in arriving. Fortunately, just as we were preparing to leave for Gangtok, we were relieved to see them arrive with the loads unharmed.

We returned to Darjeeling around the end of August.

THIRD EXPEDITION (1936)

DURING DECEMBER 1935, MAJOR [JOHN] Morris, who had been part of Mr. Ruttledge's expedition in 1933, arrived in Darjeeling and sent for Ang Tsering and me. He asked us to go to Solu-Khumbu to find porters for an expedition that would take place the next year. We found the required number of porters for him, and we were also hired.

We were now experienced mountain climbers. We had earned the rank of "tiger," and we were each given ten porters to supervise. Our daily salary was increased to one rupee and six annas, and we were given a red patch that showed our rank as section leaders. When we arrived in Kalimpong, we assigned everyone's tasks. Pasang Bhotia and I were put in charge of provisions and supplies.[10]

I had learned to inventory and number the loads myself, but Pasang could not read the numbers, so we decided not to mark his. I invented an organizational system that used four colored flags: white, green, red, and yellow. These identified each group's bundles. I told the mule drivers to stack bundles according to the color code, and I made each of them responsible for reloading at every stage.

Thus we left Kalimpong and crossed Sikkim, then continued on to Kyishong, a Tibetan village in the Shekar Dzong district. We were very hungry and thirsty when we arrived.

Norsang was the Sherpa sirdar, and he told us to go to a place that he knew to get some drinks, not forgetting to bring some for him. He insisted that we not go anywhere else, and he had a Tibetan come with us to make sure that we complied with his instructions. We were very relieved to finally be able to quench our thirst, but unfortunately we had forgotten that our loads had arrived and that the pack mules had been left alone. When Mr. Ruttledge arrived in the evening, he was very displeased and called for the sirdar to ask him who was watching the numbered loads. Naturally, Norsang said that it was me. When I returned to the bivouac in high spirits, Mr. Ruttledge gave me a stern talking-to.[11]

We stopped for two days in Shekar Dzong. After a night of heavy drinking, two of my comrades got into a brawl with the secretary of the *dzongpen* (governor) and broke his nose in the fight that ensued. They

were punished by being made to carry the maximum load of thirty-seven kilos for the rest of the journey to Everest. But we could not accept that they had to carry such a load for such a long distance, so we arranged to relieve them a little bit.

When we arrived in Rongbuk, the entire expedition went to visit the highest of the lamas, to pay our respects to him and to pay homage to the god he was said to represent. We took up a collection for an offering, and he responded by giving each of us a *sho-khang*, a Tibetan item that we kept as a talisman.

When we arrived in Shekar Dzong, the porters who had been hired for the expedition were already there, having come with Ang Tsering. We had examined the fifty men who were there, and the doctor had deemed twenty-eight of them not suitable for the expedition. Undoubtedly they thought that, because they had gone to the trouble of showing up, they would be accepted anyway. But I refused to do that, and I insisted that we dismiss the undesirables before going any farther. Our chances of success were not stellar, because it seemed that the monsoon was going to arrive very early. But despite that, we decided to make at least one attempt before the weather deteriorated. When we arrived at base camp, we delivered our loads as planned, and we each received a felt hat for the good work we had done.

We began the ascent, and set up Camps I, II, and III. For Camp II, we had chosen a location near the Camp III that we established in 1935. It was a very comfortable spot. We climbed to Camp IV, but the weather had become so bad that we were forced to descend to Camp III, and we could progress no farther.[12]

I had been assigned to take care of feeding the porters in Ang Tsering's absence, but they were constantly clamoring for food. It was an annoying and demanding task.

Finally, everything was ready for the final assault or at least to climb to Camp IV. I was asked to choose the best men. I selected Da Tsering, Phur Temba, Tsering Tharkay, Rinsing, and Pasang, who were robust and experienced mountain men. We were provided with special high-altitude equipment and promised some tantalizing rewards. At the departure time, a violent storm came up, a true cyclone that destroyed nearly the entire

camp. The route to Camp IV was impassable, and the sahibs lost hope. They expected us to do the impossible to reach Camp IV. We made three attempts to get there, but each time we failed. We had to give up and turn around for good. We were disappointed, and our hopes were dashed. We had to return to base camp and abandon the expedition.

Ang Tsering's men and my men pooled their money to give me a gift: a Sherpa scarf and a horse for the return trip, in gratitude for the way in which I had distributed their rations.

We went through the Kharta valley once again, and again we had to cross the upper section of the Arun River on the terrifying rope bridge, and this time catastrophe struck. The Tibetans who were supposed to operate the bridge from the other side were not there when we arrived. So someone had to volunteer to cross in some way or another in order to find them. Karma Paul asked Kusang Bhotia to take the risk.[13] Poor Kusang did not dare refuse, but he had a premonition. He asked Wangdi Norbu to put a piece of bread in his mouth, saying that it might be his last meal. Wangdi obeyed, while Kusang hung by his hands from the cable, which started swinging in a worrisome way. As he approached the middle of the river, Kusang seemed stuck, for reasons that I do not understand, and he could not continue any farther. One of the sahibs wanted to go and rescue him, but before he could start out, Kusang was overcome with exhaustion and let go, falling directly into the middle of rapids. He disappeared into the whitewater.

Kusang's family received a payment of three hundred rupees. He was only thirty years old and left behind his widowed mother and his younger brother. He was a brave heart, always ready to put himself at risk for others. His death cast a shadow of mourning over the entire expedition, and the return trip was a sorrowful one, saddened even more by another terrible incident toward the end.

When we arrived in Lachen, Tsering Tharkay was overcome by a crazed passion for a Tibetan woman whom he wanted to take home with him. But she left him, we really don't know why, and he was deeply distressed. He became so sick that he had to be hospitalized when we returned to Darjeeling. He was hallucinating, endlessly repeating the woman's name, and

nothing could distract him. In the end, he lost his mind completely and wasted away before our eyes. One month later, he died.

FOURTH EXPEDITION (1938)

BEFORE BEGINNING THE STORY OF my fourth expedition, may I say that I feel a bit embarrassed about telling my story? But, after all, this is an unpretentious story, told simply as I find it deep within my memory, the only journal that I was able to keep, as I do not know how to read or write.

For this new expedition, Mr. Shipton began by asking me if I knew how to cook, and he wrote and told me to go to Mrs. Odling's house in Kalimpong. She was a good woman who wanted to teach me. I went to Kalimpong with my wife and our child to learn my new profession. I didn't know how to cook at all, and I was afraid that Mrs. Odling would find me to be a hopeless student.[14] She was nice enough to put me immediately at ease, and she had the indulgence and patience of an angel. First I had to learn the name of the many utensils and the foods to be prepared. That seemed beyond my ability.

Very fortunately, I met a Sherpa friend who had already worked as an expedition cook and had noted down the names of all of the essential items. I laboriously copied them into a notebook just as my friend had done, and I tried to illustrate them with rudimentary drawings. Mrs. Odling helped me as best she could.

After two months of apprenticeship, Mrs. Odling gave me a hands-on test outdoors. She did not seem thrilled and sent me back to the kitchen to work with her own cook. But the cook was terribly afraid that I would ruin his dishes, and he absolutely would not give me the instructions that I needed. In the meantime I had decided to learn something, because I was fed up with my usual role as a porter, and I wanted to be hired as a cook for the new expedition. Whether or not the cook liked it, I spent hours in the kitchen watching him work.

Through observation and perseverance, I ended up satisfying Mrs. Odling a little bit, and I was able to be hired as a cook by the expedition when its members arrived from England. I owe Mrs. Odling a debt of gratitude for her kindness, her attention, and her generosity to my family and me. She provided us with a very comfortable material existence. She was

also responsible for procuring all of the required cooking equipment for the expedition: dishes, silverware, knives, food, et cetera—even a portable oven to make bread and cakes. But we could not bring everything, and I was terrified of not being able to provide the sahibs with the satisfaction that Mrs. Odling wanted. We were loaded to the maximum, and we left Kalimpong for "the front," near the middle of March.

We stayed in Lachen until the slopes leading to Thanggu were snow-free. Mr. Tilman had gone to Thanggu ahead of us, and he sent word that he needed a gun and ammunition to hunt the antelope that abounded in that region. When we learned that the area was so rich with game, we went there as soon as possible. There was still a thick layer of snow covering the trail to Lachen from one end to the other. Mr. Shipton and Mr. Oliver, along with Lobsang, Gyalgen, and I, each of us with a gun and some ammunition, had decided to join the hunting party that Mr. Tilman was planning.[15] Along the way, we had seen many Tibetan antelope, but they were too far away to shoot, and we had sped up the pace in order to rejoin Mr. Tilman in Lachen, where the promise of abundant game awaited.

There Mr. Tilman took the sahibs on a first hunting outing. I waited for a few hours, then, anxious, I went in search of the hunters. I found them, returning empty-handed and sorely disappointed.

On the return journey, I suddenly saw two antelope peacefully grazing about one hundred meters ahead of me. I quickly grabbed Mr. Shipton's gun with the last remaining cartridge, and before he knew what was happening I fired. The sahibs turned to look as I dropped the gun and ran after the antelope. I was sure that I had hit it. The snow was so thick and slippery that I don't know how I avoided falling, but I ran without hesitation and finally found the antelope, lying dead under a rocky outcrop. I shouted loudly for the sahibs. They found me, and we succeeded in bringing the animal back to the bivouac. We photographed the antelope, and there was a lavish feast that evening.

The next day we left for Giru, near Khamba Dzong. We went via Dong Kung. One of our sahibs was passionate about rocks, and when we arrived in Gompa Lhabu, we realized that he was no longer with us. We were

preparing to go search for him when, at dusk, he arrived nonchalantly. Since that day, we have always called him Gompa Lhabu Sahib.

From Giru we continued on to Tengri Dzong and finally stopped in Shekar Dzong for two days. The dzongpen cordially welcomed us and offered us wine and a feast of excellent Tibetan dishes. Then, in the evening, he organized a dance performance in his home especially for us. He had gathered all of the pretty girls in the village to entertain us with their dances, and I must say that they were absolutely ravishing, to the point that some of our Sherpas became secretly engaged to them. We realized this when it came time for us to leave Shekar Dzong, when the poor girls came to bid us goodbye, with cups of chang, delicious cakes—and tears.

In fact, the people of Shekar Dzong had shown themselves to be particularly welcoming. They had even organized a pony race for us. At the end of the race, a Tibetan whom I had never met took me by the hand and invited me to go drinking with him. I was not very assured. I did not want to find myself alone with him, so I asked two comrades to join us, but along the way my worries evaporated. So I told my companions to leave us alone, and I went with the Tibetan to a monastery. Once we were there, he offered me a cup of chang, fried meat, and some ghee. Shortly thereafter, he left on horseback. I would never see him again. He had told me that he had a herd of sheep and that he lived in a village near Shekar Dzong. I had asked him to think of us when we came back from our expedition, and to remember to bring us a sheep. He promised to do that, and he faithfully kept his word. When we later came back through Shekar Dzong, a nice, fat sheep was waiting for us there, as a generous gift from my mysterious one-night host.

From Shekar Dzong, we went to Tashi Dzong via the Panglep Col. Along the way we lost a bag of sugar. This was serious, because sugar is a critical food for climbers. When we arrived in Tashi Dzong, we hired a Tibetan to bring us water and light the fire. He had to work under my supervision, because I was in charge of the kitchen. When I opened my cooking box, I took out a packet of sugar for tea, but before I knew what was happening, my Tibetan assistant had grabbed it and run away.

I immediately told one of the sahibs about this, and he sent two men to the *te-ra-wa*, or village leader, to hunt down the young man. They discovered him in the te-ra-wa's stable, just as he was about to hide the sugar in a haystack. He and the sugar were both brought before the sahibs. We received the order to strip him and whip him according to Tibetan custom. The te-ra-wa's son then apologized to us and offered us a khata as a symbol of his regret for the fact that this crime had been committed by one of his men.

From Tashi Dzong, we went to Cho Dzong. There we were told that the butcher who usually supplied us with our meat had been killed a short time before. We had to do without meat for the rest of the journey. In that place there is an old monastery that was quickly transformed into a storage area for our largest items. It was easily accessible from base camp, which was established a bit beyond the Lachen valley, near the Rongbuk Glacier. For the entire journey, the trail was covered with a thick layer of snow. When we arrived in camp, we had great difficulty finding firewood. The available supply was exhausted. As the cook, I had to make sure that we were managing our wood supply. And because we needed to have tea ready at all times, I had to use coals to keep it hot. Thus the tea was too strong and too bitter, and the sahibs were furious.

The porters were also dissatisfied, and Ang Karma, for some unknown reason, had stomach pains and asked to be relieved.[16] He quarreled with Mr. Shipton and refused to give back his high-altitude equipment. He claimed that because he had to cross glaciated land he could not bear the intense cold without warm clothes. He was intractable and appeared completely convinced that he would keep the equipment. He shoved Mr. Tilman when the sahib tried to take the gear away. The situation was turning bad. As none of the other Sherpas wanted to get involved, I came out of my kitchen and spoke to Mr. Tilman, arguing Ang Karma's case. I explained to him that it would not be charitable to deprive him of his equipment, because he was sick and could not make the journey without it. Mr. Tilman was won over by my reasoning and allowed Ang Karma to keep his warm clothes. But then Ang Karma did not abandon the team. As soon as he felt better, he returned to camp.

From base camp, we climbed to Camps I, II, and III. Once we were settled in at Camp III, my duties became a bit harsher. I had to prepare all of the meals for the seven sahibs and then help them find the route to the high camps. Then I had to return to Camp III to prepare dinner and go to bed.

I had very little space in my galley kitchen, but it was the warmest place in camp, so the sahibs were always crammed in with me, stomping around in circles to warm up. This would not have bothered me if I had had enough space to maneuver, but when seven or eight people jammed into the small space, it was impossible to cook. Mr. Shipton was always interested in what I was doing, and he was always welcome in the galley. But when the whole group of sahibs followed him in, it was unbearable, and I couldn't stop myself from gesturing to show them that the food was going to suffer and that I would not be blamed. They generally responded to my complaints by laughing, and sometimes they offered to help me.

Soon we established Camp IV, then Mr. Shipton and Mr Smythe continued higher to establish Camps V and VI.[17] The Sherpas and the Tibetan porters then returned to Camp IV, but the sahibs stayed in Camp VI. One of the Sherpas, Pasang Bhotia, became paralyzed on his right side while descending from Camp VI. His face was deformed and he could not speak.

We were terribly worried about Pasang's condition. In the meantime, we received the order to take the oxygen equipment to Camp VI. I left with my comrade Nukku and we arrived at Camp V the next morning.[18] We didn't know the route to climb to Camp VI. Fortunately, Phur Temba and another Sherpa showed us the way. Only Mr. Tilman and another sahib were there, trying to make a route. Because they could not, everyone descended to Camp IV. Pasang was there, in the same condition in which we had left him and maybe even a bit worse. He had soiled his bed and seemed to be in a coma.

Because we had to return to Camp III, I told myself that we had to try to bring Pasang with us. But no one wanted to get involved, and soon I was alone with Tilman, Nukku, and Norbu.[19] Poor Pasang realized that the entire team was leaving and abandoning him to his fate. One of the Sherpas covered Pasang's face with a piece of fabric, thinking that this would ease his agony. Mr. Tilman asked me to do something for Pasang. I told Nukku and Norbu to help me try to take him and his tent down to the lower camp. But

the undertaking disgusted them so thoroughly because of Pasang's soiled condition that they pretended not to hear me, and they left me alone to try to save the poor man. The only thing I could think of was to tie his hands and feet together to hoist him on my back like a package, and to take him down like that, whatever the outcome. But it was almost more than I could manage. I was short, and I sunk into the deep snow with my load. When Nukku and Norbu, who, fortunately, had not gone very far, saw the difficulty I was having, they hurried to help me.

Another serious problem arose along the way. We had to cross a deep gorge where we risked being swept away by an avalanche. Fortunately we had a long rope, and we tied Pasang's already hog-tied body to it, leaving enough slack for the descent. Two of us held the upper end of the rope, and the third slid alongside Pasang until he reached a flat spot, then the other two slid down. Thus we continued until we reached the valley near Camp III. By that method, we were able to get Pasang to a safe location. From Camp III, we took him down to base camp in Rongbuk, where a Sherpa took responsibility for watching over him.

The weather became more and more menacing, and there was no possibility of climbing above Camp III. We soon had the impression that we would have to abandon all hope of succeeding. We were eager to descend to a magnificent, peaceful spot in the Kharta valley, where we took a much-needed rest for some fifteen days. We stopped in the middle of a forest. There we found a small pond that the local people considered sacred. Its banks were covered with red stones that must have had some religious significance. The people made us promise not to go too close to this pond, since something unfortunate might happen.

We had procured a live sheep, but no one wanted to slaughter it. We Sherpas do not kill our livestock ourselves. Mr. Shipton tried to kill the sheep with one of our *kukris* (curved-blade Sherpa knives), but he only half-succeeded, and one of us had to finish the job. We stayed in the Kharta forest for about ten days. Then we went back to base camp to pack our bags and prepare to leave for good.

We took the usual return route, and in Tista we found a bus that took us back to Darjeeling.

When we arrived, Mr. Tilman treated us to a sumptuous dinner. I will never forget Mr. Tilman, who always took a great interest in me. The last letter that I received from him is dated 1951. He told me that as he was getting old, he had given up mountaineering. In my eyes, Mr. Tilman always proved himself to be a man of great courage, with a great mind.

FIFTH EXPEDITION (1951)

IN JULY 1951, I RECEIVED a letter from Mr. Morris, informing me that Mr. Shipton was organizing an expedition that would go through the Solu-Khumbu and Namche Bazaar, right in my home region.

It had been more than two years since I had been there, and I was happy for a chance to see my family again. In addition, I was overjoyed that this expedition was under the direction of my former leader Mr. Shipton. His letter specified that he would set off on August 23, 1951, and that I should meet him in Jogbani, which was the end of the rail line from India to Nepal.

I arrived at the meeting place on August 25, and Mr. Shipton welcomed me extremely cordially. We were equally happy since we had not seen each other for twelve years. Mr. Shipton talks about this in a passage from his book *The Mount Everest Reconnaissance Expedition 1951*:

> *On the 25th, too, Angtharkay arrived from Darjeeling. He is a very old friend of mine. We had been together on eight Himalayan expeditions before the war, and I had always regarded him as a man of quite outstanding character and ability. During the past few years he had set up a business in Darjeeling organizing treks in Sikkim for visitors. But he still went on major expeditions, though now as a Sirdar, or foreman. He was on the French expedition to Annapurna, and climbed to their highest camp. I had asked him to meet us in Jogbani so as to help with the transport to Namche, and later, of course, for work on the mountain. I had not seen him since 1939, when he was just a simple Sherpa porter, though a famous one, drawing the same pay as the others and carrying the same load. Now he had graduated to a different sphere. I was somewhat apprehensive of what I would find; for success tends to spoil these simple*

*people at least as readily as it does the sophisticated. He had cut
off the handsome pigtail that he used to wear and his clothes were
distressingly smart, but I was relieved to find the same shy reticence
and the same quiet humour that I remembered so well. There was
no sign of dissipation and he looked no older; indeed, he had changed
remarkably little in the last twelve years. It was curious that, in
spite of his constant contact with Europeans, he had learnt practi-
cally no English.*

When we arrived, I went with my men to the jute-weaving shops in
Biratnagar. We were supposed to spend a few days there, distributing and
assigning our loads. A truck drove us about fifty kilometers from Jogbani
to Dharan. The road was horribly washed out from the torrential rain,
and our truck had great difficulty making progress. The wheels stuck and
slid in the thick mud, and we constantly had to stuff jute branches under
them to gain some traction. We had to stop a number of times, and I truly
thought that we would never arrive at our destination. It took an inter-
minable amount of time to cover the first few kilometers, but that was
the worst section, and then we could go a little faster despite the rain. We
arrived in Dharan in the middle of the night.

The next morning we assembled a team of coolies in Dharan and con-
tinued on our way to Dhankuta. We had barely arrived when the coolies
began to desert us. The rains had begun, and they were afraid that their
fields would be neglected. We stopped in Dhankuta for almost three days,
and we could wait no longer, so we made do with the remaining porters until
we got to our next stop in Dingla. After a great deal of effort, we only found
seventeen porters there, when we truly needed twenty-five. I suggested to
Mr. Shipton that he leave with the seventeen porters and that I would stay
behind to find more men. We learned in Dingla that Mr. Hillary and Mr.
[Harold Earle] Riddiford had returned from an expedition to the Garhwal
and were on the way to meet up with us. Thus I had the pleasure, which I
now consider an honor, of meeting Mr. Hillary.

These gentlemen had a full load of provisions with them, and we were
very grateful to them, as we feared that our calculations were a little tight.

I had decided to take charge of finding the rest of the coolies that we needed. I went to see the police inspector, and he very helpfully did what was needed. As soon as I had my coolies, I left Dingla. But after a day of walking, my young men started to complain and refused to continue. I lost another day while trying to convince them to continue to Kalung, the next village where we would stop. It was an insignificant little hamlet, which had barely a dozen residents. When we arrived, we could find only a ramshackle stable to spend the night in. To add to our misery, the door was locked, and we had to break the lock off. The stable was full of potatoes, but at least it was a roof that would protect us from the icy night winds.

The next day I went to look for help in hiring some new coolies to replace the men from Dingla, who refused to continue on. At the outset, I did not believe it was possible to find the men I needed in this small, nearly abandoned village. But luck smiled on me, and ten strong mountain men from the surrounding areas said that they were ready to come with us. I chose the six sturdiest men and freed my Dingla coolies from their loads, only keeping two of them who truly wanted to continue.

We had to cross the Goi Khaska Khola, but the old bridge had been washed away, and we wondered how to cross. Fortunately the village leader came to help us with a makeshift raft that was tied to both banks of the river. We were shaking and apprehensive, but we arrived on the other bank, where I was shocked to discover that the Kalung coolies had disappeared. I was very worried, but later on we learned that they had followed another route that they were familiar with.

When we found them, they were prostrate on the ground, shouting or moaning in pain, because they had been stung by huge jungle wasps. They had thrown off their loads next to the insect nests, and recovering them was a problem for us. One of the Sherpas who went with me put on his high-altitude climbing gear and went on the attack. He was able to grab the loads, and he set them down a good distance away. The coolies were still in pain from their wounds, and they were in no condition to carry their loads. We had to abandon them and continue on to Chatuck, a Sherpa village where a few of the sahibs were bivouacking. One of them went back with two

Sherpas to get the coolies and the loads. We finally got the whole group and the loads together in the nearest village, Pang-Kho-Ma.

We realized that some of our men had been seriously hurt by the insects: one of them had a serious injury to his eye. He had to be sent back, and I learned later that he had lost the use of that eye. We were able to treat and cure the others.

We were now in Sherpa country. In Surkey, where we stopped, there was a cholera outbreak, and we saw numerous bodies being taken away for burial. I saw a few acquaintances there, but we did not dare to eat or drink in their houses for fear of becoming infected.

Two days later, we arrived in Namche Bazaar, the main village in our region. I was proud and happy that the members of Mr. Shipton's expedition wanted to honor Namche with their visit. I went down to the home of my old friend Zimba, where I received a steady stream of visitors from all corners of the Khumbu.

We stayed in Namche for two days and then went to Tengboche, the small town with the famous monastery. Our actual climb would begin from there. On the way to Tengboche, I went to see my parents in Nu-Te. I even invited our group to come with me and offered them a meal of potatoes and curdled milk. It goes without saying that my parents were very happy to see me on one of these renowned expeditions that they had heard so much about.

When we arrived at the Tengboche monastery, we found that the lamas had already prepared our campsite. The tent ropes were of excellent quality, very solid and confidence-inspiring, and we were told that they had been a gift from Mr. Tilman on his last expedition. We stayed for two days in Tengboche, then we continued on to Pheriche, a village located about fifteen kilometers higher up the valley. There I paid a visit to my brother's stable, and he provided us with the best milk we could hope for. Then we continued on to Templa and then to Lobuche, near the Khumbu Glacier. We stopped there for two days while we looked for a spot for our base camp. We found one seven or eight kilometers farther on, just at the start of the glacier, at an altitude of 5500 meters.

The surrounding area was magnificent. We were right at the base of Pumori. But we had to collect firewood, so my Sherpa comrades and I set

off. We had found some trees that looked perfect, but when we built a fire with them, the flames spread around us in all directions. What kind of wood was this that did not burn upward but whose flames spread along the ground? Soon we understood that this was a particular shrub of which only the part near the ground dries. This is undoubtedly because of the air, which keeps the plant evergreen. The next day, while doing a reconnaissance in the Lobuche-Khola valley, we had a splendid view of the Khumbu Glacier with its ice walls shimmering in the sun. Mr. Shipton, Mr. Hillary, and I went to look for a location for Camp I. When we returned, I found my path blocked by an enormous rock covered with snow. Many smaller rocks also blocked my passage.

I tried to find a route under the hanging rock. I didn't know what to do. As soon as I pulled the small blocks away, the large rock was no longer supported and came crashing down, just as a violent avalanche released. It is a miracle that I was not swallowed up on the spot. I was saved by the fortunate intervention of another stone block, which held fast when I was thrown onto it. Before I could realize what had happened, I found myself stuck on this rock, my savior, completely dazed and disoriented. It took me some time to stop shaking and find my way back to the camp, where everyone had given me up for dead.

We had to begin establishing Camp II. Mr. Shipton and Mr. Hillary, Yu Tsering, and I were responsible for it. If I remember correctly, it was October 23. We chose a spot that the sahibs called Tom's Serac.

The weather was splendid: we saw the sun glistening on the wall between Nuptse and Lhotse. We arrived at the edge of a large crevasse. We could hear the fearsome noise of rocks falling, as if an avalanche was going to bury us.

The days were now very short, but when the sun was shining, the reflection off the ice was unbearable. The sahibs tried to navigate around the crevasse, some from the right and some from the left, but finally we had to abandon the attempts and return to camp.

On October 28, all of the sahibs, along with Pasang, Nyima, and I, set off again toward the icefall to find a way to cross it without danger.[20] Pasang and I were firmly convinced that we should give up. Mr. [Tom] Bourdillon did good work cutting steps to the top of the wall, but we felt that it

was inordinately dangerous to cross the icefall with heavy loads. Finally we refused to do so.

The group then decided to go on reconnaissance in the direction of some other mountains, specifically Pumori (7135 meters), Gyachung Kang (7678 meters), Cho Oyu (8183 meters), and Makalu (8450 meters).[21] Four sahibs headed west from base camp to explore Pumori, while Mr. Shipton took me to reconnoiter the western chain along with Mr. Hillary.[22]

Once these explorations were complete, we returned to Tengboche and from there we reached Lobuche. The sahibs decided to go to the Nangpa La, and we went with the entire team. Along the way we stopped in Thame (where Tenzing [Norgay] was born). Mr. Bourdillon and Mr. Murray continued toward the Nangpa La, while Mr. Shipton, Dr. Ward, and I, along with the Sherpa Ang Dorje, went to reconnoiter the Rongsher River. After getting lost, we had to wait for two days in Danglen for the rest of the team to return from the Nangpa La. At that moment, while we were walking through the snow, we found the footprints of the creature called "the snow man," or, in Sherpani, Yeti.

In Shugar we went inside a ruined monastery in the middle of the forest. Because we found the area too deserted, we crossed the forest by moonlight and arrived in Shokta at four in the morning. We continued wandering on until we found a group of Tibetans who accosted us and told us not to go any farther. They were the border guards and had been ordered to forbid all foreigners without permits to cross the border. I remembered a friend who had lived in Shokta a few years before, and I told them his name. That reference seemed to be enough for them, because, with a bit of persuasion and five rupees, they let us pass. We had not reached the Nepali border. There we met Mr. Dutta, from the Indian Topographic Service, who very kindly drove us to Kathmandu. There we rested for five days before returning to Darjeeling via Raxaul.

NANDA DEVI MASSIF (as represented in the original 1954 book)

PART II

· · · · · · · · · ·

OTHER EXPEDITIONS

| I |

My First Expedition
to Nanda Devi

In March 1934, Karma Paul was working as Mr. Shipton's agent, and he came to tell me that Mr. Shipton was going to launch an expedition to Nanda Devi at the beginning of April.[1] He asked Pasang [Bhotia], Kusang, and me to go with him.[2] We were meant to meet the group in Calcutta. We all agreed to go, and we set off on April 20. A good number of our comrades had been hired by the German expedition to Nanga Parbat, and Pasang and Kusang had both wanted to join that expedition as well. But I successfully persuaded them to come with me on Mr. Shipton's expedition.

We met up with the sahibs in Calcutta as planned, and we left for Lucknow and went to Kathgodam the same day. I traveled in the same [train] compartment as Mr. Shipton and Mr. Tilman, and although it was a suffocating journey, I was happy to travel in their company. From Kathgodam we drove by car to Ranikhet, where we arrived on May 9. We were supposed to finalize the preparations for the expedition at the government checkpoint.

The Ranikhet region reminds me very much of where I was born in eastern Nepal, and the entire tip of the region is part of the Himalayan chain. The jungle is the same, the vegetation is the same, and the trees are the same. There we were able to hire a dozen local

coolies, and after a day and a half of preparations we continued on the last stage by truck, traveling to Baijnath, approximately eighty kilometers away. The coolies had arrived before us. The first stage took us to the village of Gwaldam, at an altitude of 2130 meters. We spent the night there, in a goat barn, and we continued on by foot the next morning.

The next stopping point was in Joshimath, named after a Hindu hermit who withdrew from the world to meditate and pray. This village, at an altitude of 3700 meters, is now a major pilgrimage destination.

We kept going ever higher, thinking that we were going in the correct direction toward the Nanda Devi massif. In reality we had read the map incorrectly. We were going up the Rishi Ganga valley, but we had gone too far. After walking through deeper and deeper snow, we had to go back down to the valley to find the correct route, and this wasted six days. The coolies started to lose patience with our aimless wandering, we were running low on food, and we were all feeling a bit anxious. Finally, on the sixth day, we reached the confluence of the Rishi Ganga and the Rhamani, where we had decided to establish our base camp.[3] The next day we paid our Nepali porters and sent them home.

Our base camp was established on a narrow strip of cliff above the river, and we could hear the water rolling through the gorge like thunder. The cliff was hollowed out like a cave, and it protected us from the wind and snow. I served as Mr. Tilman's reconnaissance person, and Kusang filled the same role for Mr. Shipton. We were responsible for investigating the various ways of accessing the mountain. While Mr. Shipton went to explore on the other side of the river, I scaled the cliff with Mr. Tilman and then descended the south slope of the gorge. There we were fortunate to discover the Nanda Devi glacier, which allowed us to make a definitive plan for action. We were at the very foot of the mountain. The exploration had taken us a good week, and the announcement of our discovery came as a great relief to the expedition. The sahibs undertook a scrupulous reconnaissance of the area while we took care of the camp chores, cooking, and other necessary tasks. The area around us was joyous and pleasant. Herds of wild sheep wandered in the lush meadows, and magnificent flowers colored the landscape while Nanda

Devi's breathtaking peak towered above us, nearly crushing us with its glorious splendor.

But the expedition could not be delayed with reconnaissance expeditions, as the monsoon would begin in a few weeks. So we stayed there only until June 20, when the first rains began. That amount of time did allow the sahibs to complete a thorough reconnaissance of the peaks around us, and they climbed to 6400 meters. I had the chance to accompany them once and to feast my eyes on the lovely panorama of the Nanda Devi massif.

We had no choice but to put the rest of our exploration off until after the monsoon, in September. We left the Nanda Devi massif for other, easier tasks and went back to Joshimath.

We took a more direct route along the river, following animal trails, and arrived very tired, starving and soaked. My first concern was finding food, and I had the good fortune of procuring some poultry that we could cook for dinner.

We had to stay in this village for about five days, and then we set off for Badrinath, the sacred Hindu city near the source of the Ganges. Thousands of Hindus come there in every season and from all over the country. The sahibs made many forays into the foothills of the central Himalayas. They crossed many cols and glaciers, looking for the sources of the many branches of the Ganges. During this time, I was busy ensuring our material existence. I purchased a fat Tibetan goat that served as our meat for some time. I had to provide meat for all of those who were meant to serve us in one way or another: cleaners, durwans, and laborers, not to mention a large number of beggars.

At the end of July, we were still in the same area, and it was not until the end of August that we prepared to leave and cross the mountain chain from east to west. From Badrinath, we set out for Kedarnath, another sacred place, but to get there we had to cross mountains where there were no known routes. We had hired a few coolies in Badrinath, and we started to descend the Satopanth Glacier.[4] We had to cross through thick fog and deep snow. At first the glacier fell away for about three hundred meters, and then it flattened out a bit for a long way, before plunging into a deep gorge some thousand meters lower. It was an impressive spectacle, and we wondered

how we would reach the valley. The sahibs looked for a route until it was impossible to wait any longer. We had to descend with no definite plan, cutting our route through the serac fall to finally reach the flat area. There we met with a new type of uncertainty. What route should we follow over this chaotic glacier? We were now overwhelmed by the reverberations and fooled by the monotony of the expanse of ice.

Finally, thanks to the sahibs' skill and perseverance, little by little we managed to forge a route to the valley, which was not as appealing as we had imagined from above. The vegetation was so high and thick that it was extremely difficult to make progress, and with great difficulty we managed to cover one and a half kilometers per day. In addition, we had to circumnavigate many waterfalls and rapids that halted our progress. The rain fell so violently that our loads were soaked, and our food was inedible. We had no fuel for our stoves, and it was impossible to find dry wood. At times we had to take cover in bear dens, and we were afraid of being attacked.

In some places the forest reminded us of our home regions, and sometimes we could find edible plants such as bamboo shoots. We ate them for lack of other food, and we were happy to see that the sahibs were honored by the dishes that we prepared for them. Thus, our hunger was calmed for a moment, and this helped us continue on the interminable march. Bamboo is a sacred plant for Sherpas. We used it to build shelters, and we used dried bamboo pulp as fuel.

Along the way, Pasang's foot was injured by a falling rock, and he could not do any heavy work for the rest of the journey. We had now reached the bank of a large river that we had to build a bridge to cross. We had no tools other than our kukris to cut wood. We used them to cut down trees, which we felled across the river to create a rudimentary bridge.

As it was late afternoon, we camped where we were. But we were hungry, and the cooking pots were empty. Our clothes were soaked by the never-ending rain, and they stuck to our skin. We wrung them out and hung them to dry, so that night we slept naked. Our situation was pitiful. We took shelter under a rocky outcrop to cook chapattis with the *atta* (wheat flour) that we had left. We could eat only sparingly, as we were uncertain of our next meal.

The next day we arrived at a sad hamlet that had no more than four or five little huts. When the residents saw us they were afraid and ran away, but two old people stayed sitting next to their hut. As we walked toward them, they wanted to run away as well, but I assured them that we meant no harm, and that we only wanted to be their friends. When they understood that we were tired and hungry, they offered us what they had. One of them called to two villagers who sold us whatever they could: atta, a few cucumbers, a few squash. That night, we made a semblance of a meal.

The next day we discovered another small village. Because we wanted to camp in an unoccupied hut, the villagers who were returning from work claimed that it was their "relaxation house" and refused to let us spend the night there. Only the sahibs were allowed to use it.

The next morning our route took us in front of a tiny inn, owned by an old man who looked more like a hermit than an innkeeper. The inn consisted of a small bamboo hut just big enough for him, insulated with mud and sand and covered with a thatch roof. The old man was seated on a platform made of barely squared-off tree trunks, and in front of him he had a kerosene can full of *gur*, the raw brown sugar extracted from sugar cane. As we were dying of hunger, Mr. Shipton purchased the can and split its contents between all of us.

Finally we arrived at the main trail to Kedarnath. A crowd of pilgrims seemed to be going the same way. We crossed the river on a sturdy bridge and reached Ukhimar, a sizable town, which had a dharamsala and a school. We could stay there in comfort, and we found considerable supplies of food and cigarettes. The residents were very hospitable and ready to provide us with whatever they could procure. There we took on copious provisions of atta, rice, and frying oil before continuing on to Kedarnath via Mundal and Chamoli. When we arrived in Kedarnath, the town was bursting with pilgrims, and we had a terrible time finding lodging. Thanks to the kindness of a rich merchant, we were able to secure a house for the night.

Finally this exploration through the area with no trails was finished. However, the monsoon would soon end, and when September came we would set off again toward Nanda Devi.

From Rishi Ganga on, we found ourselves in familiar territory, because we had scrupulously prepared a map of this region during our previous visit. The monsoon was nearly done, and we were lucky enough to have good weather. After having thanked and released the last coolies hired, we began the climb up Maiktoli, which is 6803 meters. We set up camp at 6100 meters, just below the summit, which Mr. Shipton, Kusang, and I reached. Mr. Shipton could not tear himself away from the magnificent view that we had from there of all of the high peaks that form the Nanda Devi massif. He admitted to me that he had decided to climb Nanda Devi itself, the highest and most appealing of all of the peaks that lay before our eyes, sparkling in the sun.

We descended back down the ice slopes of Maiktoli to get back to our camp. Then, the next day, we resumed the interminable descent. There were hard, sparkling ice walls into which we had to cut steps. At every moment we feared that an avalanche might sweep us away. Finally we reached a comfortable bend that offered a good location for our camp. We had barely set up our tents, however, when the feared avalanche tumbled down on us.[5]

We spent the next day waiting for Mr. Shipton and his colleagues to make a decision about Nanda Devi. For good reason, they abandoned the attempt and gave us the order to pack up and prepare to return. During that time, the sahibs began a reconnaissance of the entire Nanda Devi massif and the surrounding mountains. We were ordered to leave all superfluous utensils and food where we were, and to make our loads as light as possible.

The descent was difficult: we were roped together and crossed steep ice slopes. Mr. Shipton led the way with me, followed by Pasang, Kusang, and Mr. Tilman. Pasang and Kusang continuously slipped and fell, and Mr. Shipton asked me to replace him for a few moments so that he could control the men who were roped together. The slopes were covered with black earth mixed with snow, which made it very difficult to walk. We sank deeply into the mud, and it was tremendously difficult to progress. We made large balls out of a mixture of dirt and snow, and we attached them to a rope to pull us downward, one after the other. Mr. Shipton agreed to go first, followed by me, then Pasang and Kusang. But Mr. Tilman refused. This was a completely original way of traveling, and I will not soon forget it.

Thus we were able to reach the next village: Sona Dhanga ("Field of Gold"). It is located on the bank of a river whose banks are said to contain gold dust. The sahibs attentively examined the sand, but I don't think that they found the least bit of gold.

In Ranikhet, we were at the end of our journey. Before we went our separate ways, Mr. Shipton asked me if I would accompany him on another expedition to Nanda Devi. With no hesitation, I told him that I would.

In Darjeeling, I learned of the catastrophe that had befallen the German expedition on Nanga Parbat, where many Sherpas had died. I would have been on the German expedition with my two friends if Mr. Shipton had not taken us to Nanda Devi.

| 2 |

KABRU

THIS WAS ONE OF MY first expeditions. In November 1935, Mr. C. R. Cooke and Mr. G. Schabarth asked me to accompany them to Kabru North. I was the sirdar for their porters, and I was in command of some thirty Sherpas. We left from Darjeeling to meet up with the other expedition members on the way to Phalut ("Phaling" in Tibetan), which required that we ascend continuously for nearly four days toward the Singalila chain, which sits at an average altitude of 3800 meters. From Phalut, we needed five more days to reach our next stage in Chubrang, near the Tibetan town of Dzong-Ri. There we rested for two days and spent our evenings playing cards, which irritated Mr. Cooke intensely. He also forced us to spend the next day in a dense forest, under the pretext of gathering wood for the journey.

We laboriously strode through this forest, attempting to get out. Finally we rejoined the majority of the group, who had followed a more direct route to the Chumbah La, a pass located at 4900 meters. It was snowing fairly hard, and the porters were becoming frustrated. After a tedious climb, we arrived on the col, on a small plateau facing the Koktang Glacier. There we set up base camp. We had a view of the snowy peak of Kabru at 7338 meters. It stood resplendent, directly before us. We set up our camp and prepared to retire to our tents for the night, when some Sherpas started spreading a rumor

that we were very near the den of one of the notorious Yetis. Panic ensued, and a hail of stones was thrown in the direction of the imaginary hideout of the mystical being. Some men shouted and clamored in a way that was as grotesque as it was useless. Of course, nothing happened, and all went back into their tents to sleep.

The next morning, the sahibs and their Sherpas set off for Kabru, leaving me in charge of the camp.

As I was alone, I fell prey to a growing terror when I thought about the Yeti, this unknown snowman, and I moved my tent into the shelter of a large rock, thinking that I would make an impenetrable fortress there. I even took the absurd precaution of barricading the door of my tent, using large blocks of rock. In front of them I arranged two towels soaked with kerosene. At the least sign of danger, I would set them on fire to scare the Yeti and cause it to run away. This is what the folklore of our people told us to do. Nothing happened to cause me any alarm, and the next day I was well rested and ready to work.

Ang Thari arrived from Darjeeling with the mail, and I took him to search for wood, as we were running low on fuel.[1] The sahibs had decided not to establish any other camps, so they planned to attack Kabru directly, starting from base camp. They set off the next morning. I went with them up to approximately 6700 meters, and then I went back to camp to resume my duties of supervisor and cook. The climb took them almost the entire day, and I waited anxiously. It was nearly six o'clock in the evening when one of the Sherpas who had accompanied the sahibs returned in a rush to tell me that they had succeeded. When the sahibs arrived a bit later, we cheered and applauded for them, and prepared to celebrate the event with a sumptuous feast. We had roast pork, curried chicken, and many different drinks. We built fires in camp and sang until we fell asleep.

The next morning, we set off on the return journey via Pemionche and Richingpong. We had to walk the entire way, nearly eighty kilometers. When we arrived in Richingpong, we were dead tired and dreaming of the copious amount of drinking we planned to do when we stopped. As exhausted as we were, the alcohol revived us to the point that we ran wild through the Richingpong bazaar, singing and dancing in the middle of the street. We

were so intoxicated that when we returned to go to bed late that night, Mr. Cooke prohibited us from entering the bungalow and forced us to sleep in the bazaar. The next morning, the sahibs forgave us for our debauchery, and we continued on, happy and gay, to Darjeeling, where we arrived the next day. Thus ended this short and pleasant expedition.

| 3 |

My Second Expedition to Nanda Devi

At the end of Shipton's 1936 expedition to Everest, it had been decided that its members would accompany Major Osmaston from the Indian Topographic Service on another expedition to the Nanda Devi massif.[1] The goal was not to climb the mountain, as Mr. Tilman had already accomplished this with his team of English and American climbers while we were on Everest.[2] But Mr. Shipton had become so absorbed in his passion for Nanda Devi that he had decided not to miss the chance to return there. Thus it was agreed that we would accompany the major and his team of photographic surveyors while they did their research.

In Kathgodam we rejoined Major Osmaston, his team, and seven other Sherpas. Along the way we met the group[3] that had just climbed Nanda Devi, and we celebrated their success.

Because we knew the route, we had no difficulty in establishing our base camp in the same location as before. The surveyors got to work, and Mr. Shipton accompanied Major Osmaston, while Sen Tenzing and I took care of the camp. Two days later, Mr. Shipton brought me with Ang Dawa to climb a 7000-meter peak. This was a difficult climb because of the deep snow and steep ice. Ang Dawa found this too difficult and abandoned the party. He left us and descended by the

quickest route. When I met up with him back at camp, I poked fun at his lack of nerve, which really got under his skin. He offered to accompany us on the next climb. Mr. Shipton had promised us that we would do as many summits as possible, and there was no shortage of peaks in the massif.

One day Major Osmaston came with us. We sank into the deep snow. Mr. Shipton's ice ax was bothering him, so he threw it on the ground a bit farther on. Major Osmaston, wanting to do the same, lost his footing and slipped into a crevasse and was badly bruised. Fortunately the crevasse was not deep, and the major had only superficial cuts and bruises, but he understood that mountaineering is not a leisure activity.

Sen Tenzing and I always accompanied Mr. Shipton on his hikes around the Nanda Devi basin, on his climbs and explorations of the massif's forests and glaciers. We climbed one of the main summits, Dunagiri.[4] From afar, the peak glowed like a mirror, shining unbelievably brightly in the sun. It was a singular mixture of rock and snow, with light and shadow playing across it and fooling the eye. Mr. Shipton bet me that I would not reach the summit. I accepted the challenge.

The next morning Sen Tenzing and I ate an early breakfast and then set out. There were so many obstacles to cross and climb over that we started to lose track of where we were, until finally we came to a snow-covered summit. Sen Tenzing had a little vertigo, and he would have slipped if I had not held him with all my strength. We immediately descended and went to Mr. Shipton to tell him that we had won the bet. But Sen Tenzing decided that he would not climb anymore.

This expedition made me very happy. It was very different from the others I had been on. This expedition was a vacation. We only attempted the climbs that interested us, and we took a great deal of pleasure in the energizing activity, the atmosphere, and the surrounding area. We had as much time as we wanted to relish the marvels and grandeur of the Himalayan world.

When we returned from the expedition via Joshimath, our usual rendezvous location, we found most of the group. In Ranikhet, Mr. Shipton met up with some friends who wanted to take an excursion into the mountains. We turned back the way we had come from and returned through the forest and along the Rishi Ganga.

In the middle of the night, Sen Tenzing and I were asleep in our tent when we were awakened by a strange noise, which sounded like a deep-voiced, growling bear. We believed that it was one of the mysterious Chokpas, or Yetis, which the sahibs call the Snowman. We both went out to see what was happening. We investigated all of the surrounding hills, and although we still heard the noise, it grew fainter and fainter until the total silence sent us back into our tent.

The next morning, Mr. Shipton took his guests up into the mountains. One of them was a woman[5] who was very passionate about the mountains. While they were gone, Sen Tenzing and I cooked and watched over the camp. We stayed there for two days, and then we packed for the return trip. We were running low on food and kept looking for a village along our route. It started to get dark, and we were still in a deserted area. We had to bivouac in a forest and look for wood to make a fire.

Sen Tenzing had climbed a tree in the dark, not realizing that he was hanging above a cliff. All of a sudden, I heard a branch crack, then the dull noise of a body bouncing down the slope. I ran to get Mr. Shipton. Together, armed with an electric lamp, we were able to find my comrade, lying in a heap in the middle of a dense bamboo thicket. Once we extracted him, we saw that he was having trouble breathing and seemed unconscious. In camp we were able to revive him only after a half-hour of effort. This accident upset me so much that I could not cook anything that night. The team had to settle for eating, raw, the few remaining grains and vegetables. I gave the coolies a little rice that they silently gnawed on. In a stroke of luck, the memsahib (the woman) had thought ahead and had brought some emergency food. She gave us a few slices of her delicious plum cake. I was very worried about Sen Tenzing. He was moaning and very agitated. I stayed near him and watched over him all night. The next morning, he was doing better. Once again he could walk along with us.

The company broke into groups again. Mr. Shipton went off with Sen Tenzing, and the memsahib took me to see the famous Taj Mahal in Agra. We visited that city and then left for Bombay, where Mr. Shipton and Sen Tenzing had arrived in the meantime. We had visited the ancient caves in Elephanta, but we had not seen much of Bombay: the riots between Hindus

and Muslims had taken a serious turn, and traffic was almost at a standstill. We accompanied Mr. Shipton and the memsahib to the Taj Mahal Hotel. There, for the first time in our lives, we encountered the luxury and magnificence of the sahibs. We wondered what the people where we came from would think of this splendid palace and the elegant life that went on there. We boarded the ship that would take the sahib and memsahib back to England. To our Sherpa eyes, this ship was also a marvel. After we watched our patrons leave, we returned, as agreed, to the Army and Navy Stores, where we were given train tickets to return to Darjeeling via Calcutta.

In Calcutta I took my friend Sen Tenzing to the museum and the zoo. He had never seen these things. On the way to the zoo, we met two men who said that they had seen us in Kalimpong, but we had no memory of them. They came along with us. As we passed in front of the Palace of Justice, they asked us to wait for them for a minute while they went to do something in the court offices. We waited outside for them for nearly an hour. As they did not come back, we became suspicious and checked in our pockets to see if our wallets were still there. Our wallets had disappeared, along with all the money in them. We had only one anna left in our pockets, and our train tickets had also disappeared.

We had to act quickly if we did not want to miss the train. I had the idea that someone at the Himalayan Club might help us. When we arrived there, we were told that the secretary was not there. Tenzing sobbed in despair and accused me of being the architect of our misery. We wandered through the city like fugitives. We were starving and our souls were crushed.

It was seven o'clock and all the lights in the city were shining, while we sat in a tram shelter, miserable and hopeless. A heaven-sent stranger approached us and asked us why we were looking so sad. We told him our story and he very kindly took us to the Hotel Sherpa. There, finally among our countrymen, we found refuge and help.

We were able to take the evening train home to Darjeeling. Sen Tenzing never forgot the Calcutta pickpockets. That day we lost two months of wages, plus the little money that we had otherwise saved.

| 4 |

My First Journey to
the Karakoram

UNTIL NOW, I HAVE TALKED about expeditions that I joined in the eastern Himalayas. I will now take the reader toward the summits to the west, which extend into central Asia. They are called the Hindukush. This great chain of mountains seems endless. It runs for a great distance through the Asian continent. It is difficult to precisely distinguish its various components, which seem to be melting one into another, in a continuous chain.

Whether the Hindukush is considered part of the Himalayas or whether it forms a separate massif I cannot say, but I can confirm that the Karakoram chain has the greatest number of high peaks in the world.[1]

In April 1937, Mr. Shipton hired me to organize the porters for an expedition that was to leave from Srinagar at the end of the month. I hired six Sherpas and left with them for Darjeeling to meet up with the sahibs in Rawalpindi. We were all on time for the meeting, and together we left for Srinagar. I really like this city for its location and its perfect climate, and I was overjoyed to visit it again.

We stayed in a tent with the sahibs in the spacious park of a resident British sahib, whose wife took care of us and provided us with excellent food. Our stay was most enjoyable. At that time it

was inexpensive to live in Kashmir. One rupee was enough to buy a sizable amount of rice or wheat flour, and one anna was enough to buy four beautiful eggs.

During the first week of May our preparations were complete, and we set off. We took pack mules to the foot of the Zoji La. Then the porters took over the transportation. It took us almost a full day to cross the pass, and we did not reach the other side until four o'clock in the afternoon. We walked across a rock field, and the landscape was terribly monotonous and contrasted dramatically with the area we had just crossed.

But soon we arrived in the fertile Indus valley, and all of the river's tributaries of all sizes irrigated a vast expanse of land. There everything was fresh and verdant, and there were impressive farm fields for as far as the eye could see. Along the river, we saw men gathering what looked like golden sand. They carried it away in baskets. We were told that when the Indus sand was melted, it produced a type of gold that was used to make very famous jewelry. We had to stop in the small town of Kargil, where there was a market. There we found two Tibetans who were selling their wine, called *roxi*.[2] We purchased a few bottles and brought them to camp. We gave some to the sahibs to taste, and they sent us back to purchase as many more bottles as we could carry. Unfortunately, we could only buy three more.

We left Kargil the next day, and it took us a week to walk to Skardu. We had to camp there for two days to complete our inventory of provisions, including tobacco. Skardu is a fairly large settlement, and because we were looking for coolies, we found the *tahsildar*, the tax collector, so that he could help us in this effort. He was very obliging and soon found us thirty coolies. Our money was converted into coins that would allow us to pay the coolies, because paper money was not used in these places.

When we left Skardu, we had to cross the Indus on a barge to reach Shigar. There we had to cross another river on a bizarre barge that shuttled travelers from one bank to the other. It was made of a conglomeration of, among other things, soccer balls and goatskins that were inflated and topped with boards that one could sit on. This quasi-raft was suspended on pulleys that ran along steel cables. When it was released, it bounced violently on the surface of the water. On rebound, it gave the passenger the distinct

impression that it was taking off. I have never since crossed a river in such a dramatic way.

Five days later we reached Askole, a small village that felt like Turkestan. The great Karakoram chain rose before us. One of the coolies stumbled and fell with his load of ghee and cigarettes. The cigarettes and melted butter fell in a heap together, both of them rendered unusable. This made me angry, and I reprimanded the man for his carelessness. He responded by threatening me with a large stick that he held in his hand. I flew into a rage, ripped the stick out of his hand, and hit him several times with it. His thirty comrades, plus a crowd of villagers, threw themselves upon me. The situation was about to turn ugly, when my six Sherpas pulled out their kukris. They also brandished their pistols. This brought our assailants back to reason. The villagers dispersed, and the coolies ran toward the village to complain to the sahibs.

We caught up with the coolies just as they were explaining the incident with forceful shouts and gestures. The sahibs looked very unhappy. They had all seven of us line up, and they sternly asked us why we had struck the coolie. I immediately stepped forward and told the story as it had happened. They told me that I should not have hit the man, even if he had completely ruined our cigarettes and our ghee, depriving us of a four-month ration of those items. We were in the coolies' country. Undoubtedly the sahibs understood how we felt, but they made us promise to avoid any quarrels in these barbarous environs, where the law of the jungle reigns. I explained the sahibs' point of view to my companions, and we resolved to be more circumspect in the future.

In Askole, we had to hire twenty-five new porters, because the true climb begins there. It was truly a brutal job to haul more than two tons of equipment and rations over such difficult mountain chains and then descend into the Shaksgam valley. The entire region that we were crossing was deserted and offered no possibility of purchasing more supplies. So we had to take enough food with us for at least three and a half months.

Add to this the grave and perilous problem of crossing river rapids on ultra-primitive bridges. Some of them had bridges in name only, made of branches tied haphazardly together with rope and gingerly balanced above

the churning water. Some consisted only of two ropes, one with loops for our feet, the other strung above for our hands. Others were only floating walkways made of tree trunks tied together, with their ends touching the banks. It was truly a terrifying test to send our caravan across these kinds of bridges, above tumultuous, rushing rivers that were eager to swallow up whatever or whoever fell into them.

We left Askole near the end of May and headed to the small village of Daiju, from where we could see the Baltoro Glacier.[3] The snow was falling heavily, but we absolutely had to keep walking. The sahibs went first, and we lost sight of them. We had trouble finding the route. We took a break to allow the coolies to cook their food. We set off again, but our porters soon showed clear signs of being nervous. As we were approaching the snow zone, they set down their loads and wrapped themselves in their blankets, refusing to go any farther. I encouraged them by giving them a supplemental ration of food and some tea that I had kept for critical situations. They looked robust, but I thought that they were not very tough. Some of them wept with fear. They lay down on the ground and refused to move. The snow continued to fall, and they pleaded with me for snow goggles. I told them that I would provide them if they started walking again with their loads. Finally, through promises and threats, I was able to get them to continue walking.

Two days later we arrived at the edge of the Baltoro, one of the largest glaciers that I had ever seen. The coolies resumed their comedy, showing that they were incapable of holding up under the effort required or of handling bad weather. The view of the glacier and the giant peaks—the highest being K2—seemed unimaginably beautiful to me, more beautiful even than the view of Everest and the other peaks in the eastern Himalaya.[4]

When we left the glacier and descended to the Shaksgam valley, the landscape changed completely. Now there was nothing but verdant fields and dense forests. Along the trail there were ruins of ancient dwellings and bones of travelers who had not survived the rigors of the journey to Yarkand. We also found shards of the pottery that these unfortunate people had used. The route was entirely unknown, and the sahibs had a great deal of trouble finding the way to our objective. The coolies became intractable, so Mr. Shipton decided to send them home. For safety reasons, he asked Lhakpa

Tenzing and me to walk with them to Askole.[5] Lobsang, another Sherpa porter, followed us for some distance, and we had gone barely a mile with the coolies when he shouted at us to stop, because he realized that the coolies had smuggled a load of food and cigarettes as well as a roll of blankets.[6] We tried to stop them, but they rushed ahead until Lobsang and I caught up with them. We had to come to blows in order to recover what they had stolen. One of them pretended to faint, in order to incite his comrades against us and escape with his stolen goods. We succeeded in bringing him back to reason by promising to return his blanket if he remained calm until the end of the journey. We made him listen so well that he asked to return to camp and be rehired while the others continued home. You can see the extent to which the coolies' moods and whims complicated our expedition.

When we returned to camp the next morning, we saw that the sahibs had already left for Yarkand, without indicating which route they had taken. Lhakpa and I had to search for their tracks. Our investigations led to a unique spot, a sort of secret paradise for wild animals. It was the summit of a hill. The spot was surrounded by luxurious grassland, which was abundantly irrigated by miraculous natural springs. There we found horses, goats, sheep, and cows living in their natural state, grazing on one of the most fertile pieces of land that anyone could imagine in this rocky world. For our little group, this was a strange discovery, like a mirage of pure, unspoiled happiness. It made a lasting impression.

Most of the group had a considerable head start on us. We were still looking for their tracks, and finally crested a col. The route to Yarkand continued on the other side. A signpost reassured us: we were definitely going toward the ancient city. But the sign gave us no information about the distance!

We saw some livestock that looked domesticated, giving us hope that we were near a village. Our hunch was true: some houses appeared in the distance, and we headed directly for them. The sahibs were already there, and they were pleasantly surprised to see us again.

Along the way, Mr. Shipton had been hunting to procure meat for us, and he had succeeded in killing a couple of wild goats. But we were short on salt, and we had to wait until we arrived in Yarkand to buy more supplies.

I went with Mr. Shipton and Mr. Tilman, Lobsang, and two coolies to do a reconnaissance of the region and look for a way to the Karakoram. On the way back, we had to cross a river that ran over a rocky bed and was not at all reassuring. I wondered how we would manage, when Mr. Tilman bravely gave us an example. He plunged into the river, but he was soon swept away by the fierce current. Fortunately he was an excellent swimmer, and he made his way to the other bank. But in the confusion, he lost his wristwatch.

From the opposite bank, Mr. Tilman threw us a rope and began to haul Lobsang and me. While we were floundering in the middle of the water, I rammed into a large stone. I was carrying a package of geodesy instruments. Fortunately, as the river was about to flow into a narrow gorge, I threw myself on a large rock that saved me from certain death. The sahibs and a few coolies rushed to my aid and were able to pull me out. I was half-conscious. Mr. Shipton himself administered first aid, and when I came to, he laid me down in his own bed. When I woke up, I was covered with scrapes and bruises from head to toe.

It snowed heavily that night. The next day we continued on our way to Yarkand, and along the way we met the sahib [John] Auden and Lhakpa Tenzing. A group of children greeted us at the entrance to the old city. We took their picture, with Lhakpa Tenzing in the middle.

As we had now exhausted our supply of salt, we wanted to buy some in Yarkand. But because we had no passports, we were not authorized to stay there for very long. Our group gathered in Gatch, where a plan for the rest of the trip was prepared. According to Mr. Shipton, the expedition had three objectives. I have excerpted the following lines from his book *Upon That Mountain*:

> *We had three principal interests. First, the section that lay between the Sarpo Laggo valley and the Shimshal pass, bounded on the north by the Shaksgam river, an area of about 1,000 square miles. Second, the glacier system lying to the north of K2. Third, the portion of the Aghil range west of that explored by Mason's expedition. The two outstanding problems in this area were to find the lower reaches and outlet of the Zug Shaksgam river, and to fix the geographical*

position of the Aghil pass which had not been revisited by any Euro-
pean traveller since Younghusband's second crossing in 1889.

We began by attacking the first of our objectives: exploring the Shimshal col. The problem was finding a suitable location for our camp. Mr. Shipton felt that we should camp near the glacier. But when we realized that it would be difficult to do that before nightfall due to the deep snow, we decided to spend the night in a rocky, dry spot. During the night, while we were in bed, the low rumbling of an avalanche suddenly began, so quickly that we didn't have time to evacuate. Boulders began raining down around us, larger and larger, more and more of them from one instant to the next, and in no time we were caught up in the cataclysm, which flattened our tents and destroyed our shelter. It was a miracle that we came through this safely.

The next morning we resumed the climb. I accompanied Mr. Shipton on his reconnaissance, while Mr. Tilman and Mr. Auden took another route. One might have thought that the snow had been groomed. We came to a rocky ridge that was completely free of snow and then continued to the opposite slope. Mr. Shipton made his observations, and we returned to camp around six in the evening. As we walked back, it began to snow heavily. We sank in up to our hips. The sahib and I were roped together, and he went first. Suddenly he disappeared into a crevasse, and I heard him splash into the water at the bottom. The rope jerked me violently. I called for Mr. Shipton, but there was no response, so I hauled on the rope with all of my strength. Little by little, I was able to hoist my companion out of the crevasse. He was unconscious and had dropped his ice axe. I could not revive him, and I had to run back to camp for help. The entire team came running. Once we were back at camp, Mr. Shipton was so exhausted that we had to put him to bed.

The next day we were both in bed and unable to move. But the rest did us good, and the day after that we were able to leave camp and resume our activities. That day we attacked a steep ridge that led to the Shimshal col. Our supplies of meat were exhausted, and we were obliged to kill some wild sheep and hares when we could find them. While we were out hunting, we met two men on horseback, armed with guns. They were Pathans, the large,

well-built people who lived in these mountains. They nodded to us and spoke a few words to us in their language, which we did not understand. We tried to make ourselves understood through gestures, and after a little while we were able to explain to them that we were low on meat. They proved to be very obliging and promised to bring us some meat the next day, along with a little wheat flour.

They kept their word, and we saw them arrive the next day with a goat and some flour. But along with them, half of the people from their village came to see us. The men and women were tall and robust. They seemed curious to observe the sahibs. They wrote down our names on a scrap of paper and told us that the *mirza* (leader) from Hunza would see to all of our needs and to our well-being. Mr. Shipton gave them fifty rupees to divide between them. They were enchanted when they left us, and they came back in the afternoon with fresh milk and a great quantity of roasted meat. Some even offered to serve as porters for us. The fifty rupees that Mr. Shipton gave them had been more than repaid by the gifts and services that they offered us.

Two days later we arrived in Shimshal, the first village that we had come to in these deserted regions. There we found a man who spoke Hindustani. He was a former civil servant from Gilgit who, for some minor transgression, had been exiled to this village. But he did not seem too distressed about it, because his house was that of the richest man in Shimshal. He received us like royalty, offering us a lavish dinner and music. His home was furnished with couches with comfortable pillows, and the floor was covered with thick, yak-wool rugs. The meal included a bounty of fruits: apricots, peaches, and apples from the Indus and Kulu valleys, pieces of roast beef, curried vegetables, and round, flat unleavened bread as large as the largest curry platters, known as *roti* in this region, all accompanied by carafes of wine and yak milk. He then called upon some wrestlers who gave us an exhibition of their talents. Before we left, the next day, he gave the sahibs a gift: pieces of fine wool flannel with which to make clothes. He seemed to be a sort of chief or king, after a fashion. Because of this, we had excellent memories of Shimshal.

June was flying by, and we very much needed to complete our reconnaissance before the monsoon, which would arrive soon. We needed to reach the Sarpo Laggo valley, where we had planned on establishing our base camp. We arrived in that wild spot on the evening of the second day, and the sahibs immediately began surveying the area. The nearest village was some three kilometers away. I set off with two comrades to take a look at it.

We came back with two jars full of good wine. The sahibs were so overjoyed by this find that they sent two messengers to get more of them. The valley was irrigated by numerous tributaries of the Shaksgam River and carpeted with tall wild grasses. From this valley one can see the entire Karakoram chain, with its culminating point, K2, shining in the sun. This mountain chain is very different from the eastern Himalayas, whose peaks are more isolated and separate. The sahibs explored the entire region while we took care of the camp chores. They finished their work in one month.

We then took a return route that brought us close to the Hunza valley. The journey was tedious, winding through dry, unstable boulders and crossing steep ridges. We reached the Hunza after walking for ten days and felt that we were entering an oasis after an exhausting journey through an arid desert. The Hunza is a splendid country, a fertile valley full of flowers, meadows, and vineyards. There we were welcomed and hosted again by the mirza, who treated us with prince-like hospitality.

After resting in Hunza for three days, we left the valley for Gilgit by crossing the Tarahal col. We could see the col from the entire Kashmir valley. A direct route took us to Srinagar, and we reached it in two days. After a brief stay in Kashmir, the expedition ended and everyone continued home.

THE KARAKORAM (as represented in the original 1954 book)

| 5 |

MY SECOND EXPEDITION
TO THE KARAKORAM

OUR PREVIOUS JOURNEY TO THE Shaksgam valley had given Mr. Shipton a first glimpse of the summits of the Karakoram, so he had resolved to return as soon as possible to that region, to finish his exploration.

In May 1939, he told me about his intentions and asked me to meet him in Srinagar, along with eight other Sherpas. Nine of us left from Darjeeling in accordance with the instructions we had received. The group included four sahibs, one of whom was a doctor, and two officers from the Indian Topographic Service.

We traveled through a verdant and fertile region divided by the Tragbal and Kamri cols, before reaching the foot of the giant Nanga Parbat massif. After Gilgit, we departed from the route that leads to Hunza, which we had taken on our previous journey, and we stopped in the village of Nagar.

The sahibs were very busy surveying the regions we had come through and the various ways to access them. Life was not expensive: poultry did not cost more than eight annas, and a sheep cost only two rupees. I cooked, and I also carried one of our loads, as we were traveling with very few supplies and had not hired coolies at the outset.

We arrived in a dry region, where there were few sources of water. The rivers flowed in deep, inaccessible valleys. The weather was very hot and we were dying of thirst. We were running out of water, to the point that we became obsessed with the search for it. When we arrived at the top of a ridge we found a goat shelter, and nearby there was a pool of dirty, yellowish water. The Sherpas threw themselves on the water and, for better or worse, managed to quench their thirst before the sahibs arrived and forbade everyone to drink any more, for fear that the water was contaminated. I was so tortured by thirst that I wanted to do as my comrades had done, but the sahibs forbade me. They gave me a piece of chocolate that would not even melt in my dehydrated mouth.

We continued walking, covering a few more kilometers before night fell. But we had still not found a suitable place, with water, where we could bivouac. We sat down and listened to the water rumbling at the bottom of the deep gorges. The Sherpa Pherinji told me that if he didn't find a mouthful of water to drink, he would die. He set down his load and went off in search of a stream. He spent the entire night looking for water, without finding any. It was truly becoming impossible to continue on if we did not find water. We had all collapsed by the side of the trail with our tongues hanging out, delirious from being overcome by thirst, when we had the extraordinary luck of seeing some shepherds who were carrying containers full of powdery snow. We threw ourselves upon them and grabbed the containers after paying them a good price. This divine intervention saved us from a very critical situation. We had just enough strength to continue on for a solid two kilometers, where we discovered a sort of pit with a bit of water flowing through it. We collected as much as we could, keeping some to drink and to make as much tea as possible, and using the rest to make flour balls that we devoured.

A few kilometers farther along, we reached a river and camped on the bank. We killed a sheep and gorged ourselves on its meat, to the extent that I had diarrhea and my stomach was upset for months. At the summit of a ridge near a village, we found large wild geese that were edible. They served as our food for several days.

One evening, after we had reached another ridge, we were preparing to set up camp, but we found ourselves without a tent, due to an error.

Unfortunately a violent snowstorm blew in, and we had to spend the entire night in a narrow crack in the rock, sandwiched against one another. Although we were sheltered from the snow there, we were very cold, and we bitterly regretted our foolish planning.

We were now deep in the heart of the glacial zone, and the sahibs were very busy preparing a map of the area. It seemed to us that it was surrounded by magnificent valleys where thousands of flowers were blooming in all sorts of colors.

While the sahibs were exploring the glaciers, there was a large snow slide in our camp, and the porters were terrified of being buried, so they went to take shelter in large cracks in the rock. The snow fell without stopping for the entire night, and we had to go to bed without eating. The next day, when the sun rose, the snow stopped and we moved our camp to the foot of the Karakoram chain.

Two sahibs, along with the porters Gyalgen and Lobsang, left on a climb. I was occupied for the entire afternoon with cooking and camp chores. At seven in the evening the sahibs had not returned, so we set out to look for them. We became more worried, but at ten o'clock they arrived one after another, explaining that they had gotten lost and had nearly fallen into a crevasse.

Two of the sahibs stayed in camp for the next few days, exploring the rest of the Karakoram massif from there, while Mr. Shipton and another sahib took me to the Panmah Glacier. The sahibs had decided to establish their camp there, to survey the surrounding area for three weeks. As I was responsible for food, I left to go hunting with two porters. I walked many kilometers with my gun but found nothing. Then I saw a deer, and luckily two does were with it. I killed two of the animals and went back with my kill late in the night, to the great relief of Mr. Shipton and his companion, who had given me up for lost. We made a sumptuous meal of venison that night, and the porters were invited to the feast.

Our camp did not have a fixed location. We had to move it from one place to another depending on the demands of the reconnaissance work. One day I found a herd of deer, and I was able to kill three of them. That provided us with enough meat for two weeks. The porters were Muslim, so

there was no reason for them not to eat meat. They gorged themselves, so much that after a few days they were disgusted by it. We were able to dry some of the meat and store it.

We then climbed one of the highest passes in the Karakoram, from where Mr. Shipton began to study the surrounding valleys. We stayed on the col for several hours, then we went back down to the valley. We passed near a large frozen lake, which was a spectacular sight. One might have mistaken it for a lake of milk.

Mr. Scott Russell was meant to meet up with Mr. Shipton, and he arrived two days later and told us that war had broken out in Europe. I was stunned. I had never taken much interest in international politics, and I could not understand the reasons for this war.

The expedition was coming to an end, so we prepared to return to Gilgit, via the Hispar Glacier and Nagir. We arrived in Gilgit toward the end of September and stayed there for a week. It was a very pleasant stay. The sahibs treated us to a performance in which one of them played the role of the Hunza queen who had arrived at full speed on horseback to congratulate us on our expedition. The parody was perfect, and we were greatly amused. On another day, we took part in a soccer game between our group and a military team. My Sherpa comrades and I had never played soccer. But we wanted to give it a try, and our legs were very bruised from kicking the ball or the other players' legs or anything else that passed within our reach.

From Gilgit, our route took us back to Srinagar and its delightful valley, where a new stay awaited us. It was no less full of distractions. We then went home to Darjeeling.

ANNAPURNA (as represented in the original 1954 book)

PART III

.

ANNAPURNA

| I |

MY FIRST CONTACT WITH
THE FRENCH EXPEDITION

TOWARD THE END OF 1948, I had met Mr. Rauhul, an attaché at
the French embassy in Delhi and a passionate mountaineer. At the
beginning of 1949, I had occasion to travel to Delhi with the Indian
governmental project to study the snow pack, and I seized the chance
to go see Mr. Rauhul.

He welcomed me in an extremely friendly manner, "You are
exactly the man that I need," he said to me, adding, "Would you like
to join a new expedition?" Turning to a man I had never met, who
was seated next to him, he said something in French that I believe
applied to me. Then he introduced me to the sahib, whose last name
was Noyelle.[1] Noyelle cordially shook hands with me, and with a
friendly smile he asked me if I would agree to accompany a French
group that was preparing to leave for the Himalayas at the beginning
of the next year. I answered that I would be delighted, because the
new French sahib had immediately won me over with his kind man-
ner. I was enchanted when I left them.

Soon after I returned home to Darjeeling, I received a letter from
Mr. Noyelle confirming that I had been hired by the French expedi-
tion, with a salary of seven rupees per day, and asking me to meet Mr.

Rauhul in Darjeeling along with eight other Sherpas, to finalize the terms of our contract and to settle the details.

I responded to this request to meet with Mr. Rauhul by bringing him my team of Sherpas. We were officially added to the staff of the French expedition after a meticulous medical examination. I was placed in command of all of the porters, and I was named their sirdar. Ang Dawa and I had to meet the French in Lucknow on April 1, 1950, and the rest of the Sherpas were to meet us in Nautanwa, the last village in India before the Nepal border.[2]

As had been agreed, Ang Dawa and I went to Lucknow to meet Mr. Noyelle at his hotel. The expedition members had not yet arrived. While waiting for them, Mr. Noyelle very kindly provided us with a car, and we used it to tour the famous city. I also accompanied Mr. Noyelle on his shopping errands in the city, and I tried to help him bargain for better prices, and to choose solid and durable items for the expedition. Indian shopkeepers are not used to being very accommodating to foreign customers, so I felt that my help was useful.

This was the case when we bought a tent to be used as the camp kitchen. The shopkeeper asked us for one hundred rupees, and Mr. Noyelle seemed as if he were about to go along with it, when I interrupted the discussion and told him that I would buy the tent for him at a better price later. And when I went back to the shop in the evening, I bought the tent for seventy rupees.

I had never seen an expedition purchase so many empty kerosene cans. I was curious to know what they would be used for. I was told that the expedition was planning to use only liquid fuel. This method was new to me but seemed excellent because of the considerable difficulty that we had had during previous expeditions, when we had to find and transport sufficient amounts of firewood. Using liquid fuel was infinitely simpler and more reliable.

From one day to the next we awaited the arrival of the French group, and I was assured that they had considerable supplies. For three days in a row we went to the airport to meet them, but in vain. On the second day, we left Mr. Noyelle at the airport and then borrowed the car to go have tea at a restaurant. When we returned, the chauffeur drove at a crazy speed. One of the hotel staff who had come with us had absentmindedly stuck an arm out the car, the arm was struck by a car coming from the other way, and he was very seriously injured. For a minute we thought his arm might need

to be amputated, and we took him immediately to the closest hospital for treatment. When we returned to the hotel, we discreetly informed the management, without telling Mr. Noyelle about the incident. Despite all of that, our stay in Lucknow was very pleasant thanks to Mr. Noyelle, who treated us extremely generously.

I would have liked to accompany Mr. Noyelle to Delhi when he learned that the group had just landed, but circumstances prevented him from bringing me. However, as soon as the expedition members had arrived in Lucknow, I was the first person who was introduced to each of them. They made a strong impression on me, both because of their appearance and their honest pleasantness. I had never met a team of mountaineers who were so kind, so athletic, and had such an impressive appearance. Although I was intimidated by their poise and their elegant clothing, I was maddened by being unable to understand their language. I wanted to tell them at least a few words, to offer them a warm welcome to the admirable country of India.

Another pleasant surprise came when I saw their supplies, their cargo of mysterious equipment and scientific instruments. I had never seen such things in all of my twenty years of climbing in the Himalayas.

Their photographic equipment was beyond anything I had ever experienced, and when we were told to pose in a group, we stood there, stupidly watching them take the picture. After the photo session, we had a memorable celebration that night.

We Sherpas especially admired the expedition leader, Mr. Maurice Herzog. We were particularly enraptured by his skin tone, a brown that was close to our own. His manners were refined and full of intelligence. His luminous eyes, his tousled black hair, the lovely form of his face that was perfect down to the very last detail, his beautifully sculpted nose, and his ever-smiling mouth made him a man whom we could not help but love from the very first meeting. As primitive as we Sherpas are, we are rarely wrong in our assessments of beauty and strength, and above all in our intuition about the qualities of the heart. Our leader immediately and spontaneously earned our admiration and loyalty.

The other members of the group may not have made such a strong first impression, but they were nevertheless remarkable men, of varying heights

and sizes. Only later did I become acquainted with all of them. The doctor sahib [Jacques Oudot] was rather heavy, but so kind and gentle. I also cannot forget Mr. [Lionel] Terray, a tall, thin sahib who reminded me of a Pathan and had the dominating appearance of those robust Afghani mountain men. He was a bit frightening at first sight, but we soon developed a great affection for him. Mr. Terray's memory will live forever in the Sherpas' hearts.

In Nautanwa we met up with the rest of the expedition, as well as the enormous inventory of food and supplies. I was able to meet the other expedition members, and it seemed to me that together they formed a lovely team of mountaineers. There was Mr. [Jean] Couzy, a tall young man with an aristocratic air, bursting with energy and unequaled strength; Mr. [Louis] Lachenal, who gave the impression of an experienced alpinist, and I learned that he was a mountaineering instructor in France; and Mr. [Gaston] Rébuffat, the tallest man in the group, so tall that we Sherpas had to crane our necks to talk to him. Then there was Mr. Marcel Ichac, the most extraordinary photographer I have ever known. In time, he became my best friend. Finally there was Mr. [Marcel] Schatz, a well-built sahib of average height, who seemed to do everything, even Himalayan climbing, with intensity. The only concern in our relations with our new sahibs was our respective ignorance of each other's languages, which is always a serious obstacle to mutual understanding. However, we felt safe under their command, and for my part, I had full confidence that their efforts would succeed.

Not only were the expedition members high-class men, they also had the most modern and most scientific equipment for the high mountains. We definitely had the impression that these men were the greatest specialists who had ever attacked the Himalayas.

The Sherpa team included my most time-tested friends. Along with young Ang Dawa, the baby of the team, there were Ang Tsering, Dawa Thondup, Sarki, Fou Tharkay, Aïla, and Adjiba.[3] They were all veterans, and they contributed remarkably to the expedition's success. They were men of grit and courage.

We were now all gathered in Nautanwa, ready to cross into Nepal. From there we would cut through the very heart of the country to reach the Miristi Khola, and farther on, Tukucha, where we had decided to set up our primary base camp before leaving for Tilicho Col.

| 2 |

EN ROUTE

IN NAUTANWA, WE RECEIVED OUR marching orders. As I was in charge of transportation, I distributed the expedition's food and equipment loads over the four trucks that the Nepali government had provided to us, and, accompanied by Ang Tsering, Dawa Thondup, Sarki, Fou Tharkay, Aïla, Ang Dawa, and Adjiba, I left with the baggage for Butwal, which was the first stage on our journey to Nepal. Two sahibs had gone ahead to hire coolies so that we could progress beyond Butwal. The maharajah had sent one of his officers ahead of our caravan to help hire coolies and then accompany the expedition. This officer soon became our friend. He made things much easier for us during the entire trip.

Butwal is a very large village, and there was a large crowd there. We had arrived in the middle of a *mela* (fair). There were many shops, and everywhere people were serving tea. When they saw the sahibs and our equipment piled in the village square, the tea sellers, or *chai wallahs*, offered us cups of hot tea to grease the wheels of business upon which they depended. Some of my Sherpas drank up to ten cups. I found this excessive. That type of consumption did nothing good for our health and our work, and in addition it encouraged my people to spend money. I told Ang Tsering about my concerns, but he only laughed, and the "tea orgy" had no negative repercussions.

During this time, the Nepali officer G. B. Rana was actively working to hire coolies for us. I had to separate them into teams that were each commanded by a Sherpa. The sahibs then worked to distribute the mountain clothing, the likes of which I had never seen during my previous expeditions. Wool shirts and pullovers, thick, wool-lined suits, of such high quality and so elegantly designed that each of us was overjoyed and incredibly proud to be granted such equipment.

During the evening, the sahibs began distributing rations such as we had never tasted before. We told ourselves that France must be a remarkable country to produce such remarkable dishes with such an exquisite taste. There were cakes of many shapes, sizes, and colors, and what the sahibs call "nougat," which we called *badam mitaï* (almond candies), multiple varieties of meat and fish in boxes with amusing labels, and cookies in varied shapes and flavors. It was much too complicated for me to do a meticulous inventory, but it was all absolutely delicious, to the point that we could not stop talking among ourselves and saying that with such food, we surely could not fail to reach the summits of the Himalayas, Everest included.

When all of the loads had been prepared, we gathered for the night in a government bungalow on the edge of Butwal, where we stayed until the next morning. The first task before us was to continue uphill to Tansing (Palpa). Along with the sahibs, I was provided with a horse to ride. The coolies and the mules walked ahead of us.

Sarki and Fou Tharkay were provided with guns to guard our money, which was in Nepali coins. The funny thing was that neither of them knew how to use a firearm, and they were not given any ammunition. But no one would have dared to attack us after seeing the guns and the resolute demeanor of our Sherpas, who were actually primitive villagers without a shred of malice, from the least-visited region anywhere.

My horse was an odious nag who absolutely refused to walk unless I dismounted and led her by the bridle for a while, in order to get her used to following the line of better-built horses.

We arrived in Tansing and set up a huge tent on land owned by Tarikhel, a sort of *maidan*, or esplanade, in the middle of the village. The French and Nepali flags were hoisted to the top of some tall bamboo poles. A crowd of

onlookers had gathered, thinking that we were a circus and wondering about the show that the sahibs were going to put on for them. But they were soon disappointed when the sahibs left camp to go climb a small mountain nearby and do a reconnaissance of the region. As the gawkers grew tired of waiting for a show that wasn't happening, they dispersed and left us to continue setting up camp in peace. The next day, as we were getting ready to continue on our way, some of the Butwal coolies deserted us, and we had some difficulty replacing them. But the Nepali officer who was with us arranged to fill the empty slots, and that allowed us to continue on that same day.

When we passed through Ranighat after crossing the Kali Gandaki, the porters went on strike and refused to go farther. The sahibs were very annoyed, and I started to lose patience, but the coolies were intractable. They absolutely would not hear of going on until Rana, the Nepali officer, made some intense arguments to their leader and inflicted some severe punishment on him. All of a sudden our crew returned to reason and took up their loads, but these coolies continued to cause problems at every turn. They constantly dragged behind and caused me a great deal of concern. But I could not do much to scold them, because I was absorbed in my cooking duties until the day when Mr. Herzog decided to put Pansy in charge of the kitchen and asked me to take full charge of the coolies.[1] After that, I managed to get most of them to follow along more expediently, but I had a great deal of trouble getting the more recalcitrant ones to pick up the pace.

While we were walking along the banks of the Kali Gandaki, the coolies suddenly stopped, set down their loads, and began to bathe in the river. I waited for some time until they had finished, but then I saw them stretch out on the banks and prepare to spend the night. Fou Tharkay and I tried to rouse them a bit, but we ended up realizing that they definitely wanted to eat. We had to persuade them to continue to the next village, where we could prepare some food. After a prolonged discussion, they finally agreed to continue on, and we were able to reach the village just before night fell. After giving them the rice intended for them, Fou Tharkay and I chose a large tin of canned pork for our own meal. But our five Sherpa comrades soon accosted us and insisted on sharing our pittance, which was barely sufficient for two of us. Ang Tsering (Pansy), who was the sahibs' cook, and his

brother Aïla, who claimed not to have eaten since the day before, snatched most of it for themselves.

We were now in the very heart of Nepal, on our way to the first slopes of the mountains, and we were approaching the valleys carved out by the rivers that flow down them and then drain into the major river, the Kali Gandaki, not far from Baglung, our next stop and the final Nepali village of any size before our base camp in Tukucha.[2] We spent the night in Baglung, and very early the next morning I heard the sahibs rushing out of their tents and shouting. I did the same. They were in a state of high excitement, pointing at a blindingly white peak that towered high above us in the distance. I could only make out one word: "Dhaulagiri." For nearly half an hour, we contemplated the mountain with amazement, and we discussed routes and access methods.

We stayed in Baglung for two days, particularly to hire more coolies, who were becoming a more and more serious problem for us. Because this was a task specifically assigned to me, I had to spend most of my time on this. Another problem was water, which was scarce. We had to hire two women to go collect water from the nearest wells.

The sahibs took the greatest possible care with our food. They were insistent that we stay in good health and conserve all of our energy for the exhausting climbs that we were going to undertake. They made us eat as much poultry and eggs as we could obtain.

Because we also had to pay the Palpa coolies who refused to go farther, there was a great void in our money bag. We urgently needed to refill our treasury with Nepali coins. This was not very easy in the bazaars and villages in the region.

The local coolies we hired were more robust and resilient than their predecessors. Some could carry up to seventy-two kilos. We were stupefied and very relieved to have found such strong and willing men. As soon as we resolved the porter issue, we left Baglung and headed upstream along the Kali Gandaki to Beni, where it joins the Mayangdi Khola.

From there, we continued up the Kali Gandaki and arrived at the confluence with the Miristi Khola, near the village of Dana. Along the way, the doctor sahib had treated an old woman who seemed to be an important

person, because she gave all of us a generous amount of milk curds. In Ghasa, a small village at an altitude of about 2000 meters, the sahibs were once again delighted when they saw the high mountain peaks reaching into the clouds. Our next step was to cross the Lete jungle. Our sahibs were greatly pleased with the wooded part, and one of them, our *Bara Sahib* [expedition leader Herzog], told me that it reminded him of the mountain forests in his home country.

After Lete, we came out onto a barren, sandy plain dotted with stones and gravel, and the wind howled against us constantly. This made it very difficult and painful for our coolies and us to walk. But soon, only a little farther on, I saw prayer flags whipping on the roofs of houses. I was overcome with excitement and shouted to Bara Sahib, who was walking alongside me, "There is Tukucha!" while pointing to the village that we could see some distance away. Before we arrived there, we had to cross the tempestuous waters of the Dambush Khola. Fortunately the river level was fairly low at that time, and we crossed without incident and arrived in Tukucha.

The village reminded us very much of our own Sherpa villages: its appearance, the houses, food, drinks, surrounding vegetation, and the Buddhist temple were all similar to our own. Due to this, we felt completely at home. We felt a bond with the people who lived there, who celebrated the same festivals as we did and who dressed in somewhat the same way.

Now we needed to set up our base camp. The sahibs showed us how to open the bundles and distribute the food and many pieces of equipment. We had a great deal to do, to set up the tents and kitchens and sort out the many supplies. The sahibs joined us and put their noses to the grindstone. When it came to work, they made no distinction between themselves and us. This was a new and very pleasant experience. This way of working filled us with enthusiasm. Never, on any expedition whatsoever before, had we felt such a sense of freedom and closeness with the sahibs. We felt a bond of camaraderie between us.

There was an old monastery near the camp, and the sahibs got in the habit of respectfully listening to the prayers that we chanted early in the morning when the temple gong sounded.

The morning after we arrived, as soon as the camp was set up, a large crowd gathered to look at us. It seemed that they were Tibetan pilgrims. They were counting on a generous offering from the sahibs, so they put on a demonstration of their religious dances for their benefit. We were very grateful to Bara Sahib for the money that he generously distributed to them. This was a fortuitous windfall for these people.

Mr. Herzog then took two of us to do a reconnaissance of the area around Dhaulagiri. Mr. Ichac accompanied us and we set off via the Dambush Khola valley, through a thick jungle where we climbed steep slopes.[3] I had not carried loads since 1940, and I had lost the habit of wearing mountaineering shoes. We had no crampon straps and instead we had to use rope, which I found very unpleasant. I had also gotten out of shape due to lack of practice, which caused me to lag behind a bit. When we arrived at an altitude of 3400 meters, I couldn't go on any longer. We had just reached the snow line, and I realized that now the true climb was beginning. After the sahibs had done a general reconnaissance of the area and written down their observations, we returned to camp in the evening. We had tea and rested comfortably that night.

The sahibs used countless pieces of equipment that we had never seen: alcohol stoves, waterproof cigarette boxes, and marvelous skis, which we tried for the first time in the Himalayas. How we wished that we knew how to use them!

The Sherpas were faithful to their habits and never stopped arguing. Adjiba accused me of stealing some boxes of cigarettes, and after he had drunk a few glasses of alcohol he turned aggressive. A moment later, Aïla joined him. I lost patience and would have fought with them if Mr. Noyelle had not come and separated us. He told them that they must show more respect toward me, as I was their leader. We all ended up smiling and fell into each other's arms, and then my comrades hauled me away to drink with them. We were definitely a tightly knit group, like a big family with the sahibs as parents.

| 3 |

RECONNAISSANCE

THE TIME HAD COME TO do our initial reconnaissance, and Mr. Herzog divided us into two groups. We had reached a fairly high altitude, and the sun had begun to beat down unbearably. Schatz Sahib and his team of Sherpas left to explore access to Annapurna but soon came back, declaring the route impassable and totally devoid of water sources. The peak of Tukucha shimmered directly in front of us, with its slopes completely covered with melting snow.[1]

I accompanied the sahibs, Mr. Herzog, Mr. Ichac, and Mr. Terray, who were going to look for the "unexplored valley" on the other side of Mount Tukucha.[2] From there they hoped to get a view of the Dhaulagiri massif. After a few hours of clambering up and down at the summit of a plateau, Mr. Terray was exhausted and went back down. I followed him in the late afternoon.

A ferocious wind was blowing, and along the way we had to take shelter in a little hamlet. Mr. Herzog and Mr. Ichac stayed there with a little tent, determined to continue their exploration the next day.

In the morning, I met back up with them and found them fighting desperately to reach the top of the ridge. We had to climb for the entire day in extremely tough conditions, fighting a terrible headwind, with sleet and snow. I was concerned to see them so tired, and insisted on helping them carry their bags and lighten their loads.

They were clearly happy to see me, and together we returned to Tukucha that evening.

The next day we set off again, arriving in a village called Tringtchuk, which means "Deep Water." The village is near a small but very deep pond that is held as sacred and is visited by many pilgrims every year. Its water never freezes, even though it is on a ridge at nearly 4900 meters, surrounded by year-round snow.

Our group was composed of three sahibs, Fou Tharkay, Sarki, and me. Wherever we turned, we saw only gaping crevasses and tall cliffs of ice that waited menacingly for us. But the sahibs were extraordinarily skilled in chopping away at the steep ice walls with dangerous seracs hanging over them. I had never seen instruments or tools like the ones that they used, and we Sherpas stood in constant admiration of the bravery and skill with which they used their crampons, ice axes, and skis. In my entire life I had never seen more expert climbers. We were stupefied by what they accomplished in the fearsome and unexplored mountains.

After a long climb, we saw the village of Manangbhot, which was the sahibs' main goal in their future search for an access route to Annapurna.

When we returned to base camp that evening, the sahibs were very animatedly discussing what they had seen, while my comrades and our local Tibetan friends prepared a feast.

The next day, the Baglung lama came to see us. He was a very holy man who had the gift of prophesying the future. The sahibs called me to translate his words, and they were very interested in what he had to say to them. Mr. Ichac had asked him if they would succeed in conquering Dhaulagiri. The lama assured them that they would do better to abandon that attempt and try to attack the neighboring mountain. He was referring to Annapurna, which towered just above the holy place of Muktinath. These predictions made a deep impression on the sahibs.

The next morning, Pansy went with one of the sahibs, who was going toward Muktinath, while Mr. Herzog took me on another reconnaissance. When we returned in the evening, Mr. Herzog gave me a magnificent pair of binoculars as a gift and taught me the only French word that I know:

Bonjour. I think that this is a way of greeting the people that one meets, and I have used it ever since.

The sahibs were working diligently to find an access route to Dhaulagiri, and I once again went with Mr. Herzog to do a reconnaissance of a potential new route. But the slopes were in such a condition that we could not go very far, and at the end of the day we gave up. This failure convinced our leader to go against the opinions of the other sahibs, to trust the lama's advice and to attack Annapurna from the holy place of Muktinath.

Mr. Herzog decided to leave for Manangbhot with Mr. Ichac and Mr. Rébuffat, Fou Tharkay, Pansy, and me, along with a few Tibetans. Toward the end of the afternoon, we arrived in the little village of Thiningaon. Although the people who lived there were poor, they were clearly delighted to welcome us. They brought us to the village leader, who took us into his home for the night. There was a very strong odor there, and the sahibs became sick and were gagging, to the point that Mr. Ichac threw all of the windows open.

I began to prepare a meal for the sahibs. I set everything up outside, with the plates, the spoons, and forks, and the villagers came to watch us eat. They were intensely curious and laughed energetically. It was the first time that the sahibs had tasted our *panir* and our flat, unleavened wheat bread, chapatti. They found it delicious, and they often asked me to prepare it for them afterwards.

The Sherpas had been provided with crampons to walk on the ice, but we were very bad at using them despite Mr. Lachenal's efforts to teach us. We carried them on our shoulders and followed the sahibs to the Great Frozen Lake. There a seemingly insurmountable barrier rose before us, and we saw the sahibs attempting to decide what to do. Mr. Herzog organized us into two rope teams and broke trail across the lake, and then he led us safe and sound to the other side.

Then came a climb up Tilicho Col, at approximately 5000 meters. From there we could see a number of blindingly white 6000-meter peaks. The sahibs spent some time trying to identify them, then Mr. Herzog and Mr. Rébuffat, along with Fou Tharkay and Pansy, set off in the direction of Manangbhot, leaving Mr. Ichac and me to do a reconnaissance of the

Muktinath chain. We reached an altitude of 5500 meters, where the sahib took a number of photographs. During that time I busied myself building a cairn to commemorate our exploration, then we returned to camp in the evening.

After a good night's sleep, we climbed back to the same col and then went farther, as far as possible toward Muktinath Himal, up to about 6200 meters. I will never forget that morning, when Mr. Ichac, overcome with enthusiasm, grabbed me and shouted, "Do you see? Do you see? Annapurna! There it is, Ang Tharkay, we've found it! Come, now let's go back to camp."

And we hurried back to camp to announce our discovery to the rest of the expedition. But we couldn't do that until the next day, when Bara Sahib rejoined us upon his return from Manangbhot.

The next day I went back down to our camp with the porters, leaving the sahibs to follow us a little later. Along the way, they found Dawa Thondup splayed out alongside the trail, completely drunk, with a bottle of wine next to him. When they questioned him, he told them that he had gotten the bottle from Fou Tharkay. He refused to return to camp and instead preferred to spend the night in the neighboring village. At least this incident provided the sahibs with an explanation of why their liquor was rapidly disappearing.

We were satisfied that we had finally located the route to Annapurna, and we celebrated that evening. It seemed that the prayers I had offered at the monastery were finally being answered and that the *pujas* (religious services) that we Sherpas had conducted in our tent had finally reached the gods. Before that I had sometimes doubted whether we would succeed.

It is true that Mr. Herzog had joined us in praying at the monastery. The head lama was not there that day, when the ceremony had been performed by his vicar, and I remember that Bara Sahib had been very generous in his offering. Instead of using the usual offering of two rupees that I had advised him to make, he had emptied his pockets of all the money he had, for the temple. Now I was convinced that God wanted to thank him for his faith and generosity.

Thus we had found Annapurna, but the sahibs had to find a possible and safe access route. They discussed it among themselves, and then Bara Sahib called me to explain the plan of attack.

Mr. Lachenal, Mr. Terray, and Mr. Schatz formed the lead group, along with Adjiba, Ang Dawa, and Dawa Thondup. I was to set off with Mr. Ichac, Mr. Noyelle, and the doctor sahib the next day. Our base camp was now humming with activity. Everyone was furiously preparing for the climb, loading the bundles and sleeping bags onto the small horses that had been provided to us.

We held tight to the greatest possible hopes while loading our little pack animals, and while we set off at a little trot in the direction of Tukucha, the villagers assembled joyously, and each of us was given a *saïs*, or stable boy, who trotted alongside the pony that he was responsible for.

Before we set off on our reconnaissance of the access to Annapurna, Mr. Ichac and the doctor sahib insisted on taking me with them to visit Muktinath. At that moment, I considered it a good omen to visit such a holy place. We rode along the banks of the Gandaki River and arrived in the village of Dhabar, where we spent the night. The next morning we continued on to Muktinath via a meandering route, arriving around noon. After leaving our horses in a sort of stable, we reverently entered the town on foot. We passed before the sacred rock where it is believed that Buddha prayed, and where he allegedly left a footprint. I prostrated myself. Then I went to the Temple of Fire, where I filled my canteen at one of the sacred fountains, remembering to drink a mouthful from each one.

In the city, the sahibs visited each temple with great interest, especially the largest one, where the mystical river flows. It comes from an ever-flowing source in which it is believed that the Master usually bathed. We were welcomed by the priestesses who sang and danced for us. I thanked God for having given me the chance to make a pilgrimage to our holy city. I had the pleasure of meeting someone there I had known for a long time: a *lamini* (woman lama) who I had met at the Rongbuk Monastery, where she was studying under the high lama. She was now living in Muktinath with her mother and brothers, whom I had also met in Rongbuk. They welcomed me most cordially, offered us food, and gave our horses some forage. We stayed with one of the richest residents of Muktinath, where we were treated most congenially during our entire stay.[3]

The sahibs took photos of the temples and the women. At first, the women were a little timid, but I was able to convince them to be photographed, as long as they each received a copy of the picture. In Muktinath there was also a Hindu temple and a dharamsala where pilgrims can find lodging and food for free.

Tradition says that a long time ago, God caused a rock to rise up between two crevasses some one hundred meters behind the temples. One of the crevasses symbolizes virtue and the other symbolizes vice, and the rock is called Mélong, which means "mirror," the eye of Jamaraja, the scale of good and evil. We collected a bit of water from the streams that ran from the rock, and we bottled it, to be used as holy water. That night was a new moon, and most of the villagers went in a procession to the temples with lit candles. Then they gathered on the rock with their candles glowing. The new moon symbolizes the three powers of fire: Do La Mebar, the fire on the rock; Chhu La Mebar, the fire on the water, and Sa La Mebar, the fire on the ground. The faithful believe that a flame burns on the rock on new moon nights, but when we visited the rock, the flame seemed not to be burning. We were told that it had not burned for a year, because of the cruelty of humans who had offended Lord Buddha with their sins. The Master had extinguished the flame. Some years later, a Sherpa coming back from Muktinath had told me that the rock was once again burning on new moon nights, which had led to great ceremonies in the holy city.[4]

During our visit, the new moon festival was celebrated only with dances and songs, which brought back memories of many things that happened in our home country. We were overcome by a desire to join the dance, but it was impossible with our heavy shoes. The sahibs were interested in everything and were very generous in their offerings.

When we moved on from Muktinath, we headed toward the village of Beni, where we spent the night with one of our friends who had lived in Darjeeling and Kalimpong. A group of women and girls came to his house, and they were rather friendly with us. The sahibs were amused by this and were sure that I was an accomplished "ladies' man." That could not have been further from the truth, as I had always done everything possible to

keep my distance from the opposite sex. But we spent some pleasant time in Beni, and I am sure that the sahibs also fully enjoyed themselves.

We returned to base camp in Tukucha. During that time, Bara Sahib, along with Mr. Lachenal and Mr. Terray, had set off to search for an access route to Annapurna. The next day we learned the great news: they had discovered the route that we needed to take! Bara Sahib had sent a letter to Mr. Noyelle and Mr. Ichac, from where he was in Camp I, near the Annapurna glacier.[5] In the letter, he stated his intent to attack the mountain and said that he was certain that we would succeed. He told us not to waste a single instant, and he gave specific instructions to each sahib.

This news caused great excitement, and in our base camp everyone began actively preparing for the assault. Sahibs and Sherpas immediately began to pack up our things and the climbing equipment that we needed, and everyone started doing exercises to get back in shape. After the assault team had left, only Mr. Noyelle and I remained in Tukucha. Along with my companion, I then took care of putting everything in order at base camp: there was no more cleaning or organizing to be done. Thus we waited in Tukucha for new orders from our leader.

| 4 |

THE ASSAULT

IT WAS NEARLY NOON, ON a day near the end of May, when Sarki came running from base camp with an urgent letter for Mr. Noyelle from Bara Sahib. When I saw Sarki's face and how exhausted he was, I realized that he had run to us as quickly as he could and that he was bringing us important news. Once Mr. Noyelle had read the message, he called me and told me to assemble as many coolies as I could, with all of the equipment that the sahibs needed for Camp I. I lined up twenty-four coolies with their loads and, guided by Sarki, I led them to Camp I, where I turned the coolies and the equipment over to Mr. Ichac. Then I returned alone to base camp.

When I arrived, I found Adjiba, who told me that Camp III was already established.[1] This was excellent news, because I was not expecting to see the sahibs progress so quickly over such difficult terrain and challenging, glaciated slopes.

"But, why did you come back?" I asked him.

"Oh!" he answered, clearly terrified. "The sahibs made Aïla, Sarki, and me climb a horrible ice wall, and they wanted us to cross a terribly deep crevasse. I was shaking in fear, and I asked to turn around. Aïla and Sarki had gone ahead, and they were able to cross over with the sahibs' help. But the sahibs wanted to send me back, to shuttle loads between base camp and Camp I."

I berated poor Adjiba for his lack of nerve, but the poor man truly seemed to have momentarily lost control of himself.

The next day, I went with Mr. Ichac to Camp I. He told me to accompany some Sherpas and porters who were carrying loads to Camp II.[2] There we found Mr. Herzog, who had returned from Camp IV.[3] We met up as planned, and Bara Sahib gave me a quick summary of the progress that had been made on the assault. I updated him on what I had been doing for the past few days, and I told him about my propitious visit to the holy city of Muktinath.

"I prayed fervently for our success," I told him. "I am sure that God heard my prayers."

Our leader seemed happy to have me near him, and I felt exactly the same way. Night had fallen, and the view was glorious and deeply moving. Annapurna's summit looked like a crown of flames that was gradually fading. We were at nearly 6000 meters.

I had never seen anything like the ascent from Camp II to Camp III in my twentysomething years of climbing, and neither had my comrades. Bara Sahib, Mr. Lachenal, Sarki, and I had to continually cut steps into dreadful ice walls. Without the complete confidence that I had in the sahibs, I would never have dared to risk such a route. But when we arrived at Camp III, we were completely healed by the comfort of the camp. We immediately started preparing a meal, and after that we spent a restful night.

The next day, we set off for Camp IV. Sarki was roped up with Mr. Lachenal, and I was with Mr. Herzog. Camp IV-A was located on what they called the Faucille Glacier. Once the camp had been set up, Mr. Herzog told me to descend to Camp IV, 200 meters below, at the foot of an ice slope, and to find the tent that we had left there and bring it up to the new camp the next morning. It was nearly dark, and Sarki and I had to descend the ice steps that we had just climbed up. But now I was used to chopping at the ice, and the descent proved to be easier than the ascent.

The next day, we climbed back up to Camp IV-A with the gear. There Bara Sahib and Mr. Lachenal decided to establish Camp V the same day, and a few hours later we left Camp IV-A to accomplish this. It proved another arduous climb, even more exhausting than the previous one. The

wind, loaded with snow, blew more and more violently as we fought to cut steps into the steep slope. Now we could clearly see our objective rising above our heads. The snow was so deep that we sank up to our waists. With each step, we wondered apprehensively whether it would be our last, not only because of the risk of being buried but also because of the effort that our hearts and lungs were putting forth. Finally, after a nearly superhuman battle, and thanks to the sahibs' extraordinary determination, we reached the spot that had been selected for Camp V.

The sahibs were looking for a possible location for the tents among the icy ridges and slopes covered with hip-deep snow. It was impossible to find a surface that was sufficiently level to set them up. We had reached an altitude of 7300 meters, and we continued to climb, completely out of breath. The snow and wind were horrific. When we had climbed some 200 meters higher, the sahibs began chopping at the ice. We were terrified of ice blocks crashing onto us, or an avalanche sweeping down.

After chopping a niche in the ice for the tent, the sahibs decided to set up Camp V there. Then Bara Sahib called to me to ask if I wanted to do the final climb to the summit with him. He had decided to start the next day. I was wholeheartedly with him in this magnificent undertaking, and the idea of abandoning him at the moment of the supreme test seemed repulsive to me. But my feet were starting to cause me pain, and I was horrified at the thought of seeing them freeze. I looked directly into the determined face of my heroic leader. Alas! I was shirking my duty because I was not worthy of sharing that unequaled honor with him or the just reward that his courage and sacrifice would merit.

"Excuse me, Bara Sahib," I said to him pitifully. "But I am not worthy of this great task. I am profoundly grateful to you for the honor you have given me, and in all my life I will never forget this moment. Allow me to return to Camp IV-A, and may God protect you, you and the valiant Lachenal Sahib!"

With those words I left our brave and noble leader, and, confused, I quickly descended to Camp IV-A with Sarki.

Early the next morning, while we were still sleeping at the intermediate camp (IV-A), two sahibs, Mr. Rébuffat and Mr. Terray, and four Sherpas

arrived. They were going to meet Bara Sahib and the assault team at Camp V. Pansy and Aïla were part of the group, and they asked me to go with them, but I told them that I had just returned from Camp V and that the final assault on Annapurna was supposed to happen that same day. They told me that they would leave the sahibs at Camp V and come back to Camp IV.

After they left, Sarki and I descended to Camp IV in search of greater comfort. During the afternoon, our Sherpa comrades came back from Camp V, and we all drank some tea together. The next day, there was a huge snowfall, which made us fear that there would be an avalanche. It began well before dawn, and when we woke up, we found our tents completely covered. We had to crawl out and clear the snow off. Fortunately, we were able to find a kind of fracture in the rock, and soon we were able to shelter all of the tents and equipment there. It also protected us somewhat from the snow that was falling incessantly.

We spent the entire day and night blocked in by the snow squall, held prisoner in our cave. Our morale was very low, and we could not stop thinking about the sahibs who were trying to conquer the fearsome Annapurna, exposed to the snow, cold, and wind. We were very worried about what would happen to them. Our hearts were with them, and we prayed fervently that they would be protected and that they would succeed. The snow was still falling hard, and huge blocks of snow and ice were raining down on us. We thought that we might be buried at any moment. Thus, we spent some terrifying hours. We couldn't do anything other than lift our thoughts up to God to implore him to protect us.

What was happening up on the mountain? We were crazed with anxiety and could only wish for the worst not to happen.

| 5 |

VICTORY

FROM THE EYEWITNESS STANDPOINT, I cannot say anything about
the greatest accomplishment in the history of mountaineering: the
conquest of the 8075-meter peak of Annapurna on the first attempt.[1]
But I am nonetheless proud that, during my career as a Sherpa, I was
among those who in some way were part of the conquerors' triumph.
It was right that it was the expedition leader who planted his coun-
try's flag on the summit, but the most enthusiastic of the sahibs was
with him at that moment, and the entire expedition was united with
them throughout the vicissitudes of this great adventure.

In quoting the words of our great leader, from his book about
Annapurna, I can only honor him by saying that we Sherpas
believe that he deserved the homage that we, humble Himalayan
natives, gave to him, one of the greatest alpinists whom we had
ever served:

> *My joy was touched with humility. It was not just one party
> that had climbed Annapurna today, but a whole expedition.
> I thought of all the others in the camps perched on the slopes
> at our feet, and I knew it was because of their efforts and
> their sacrifices that we had succeeded today. There are times
> when the most complicated actions are suddenly summed up,*

distilled, and strike you with illuminating clarity: so it was with
this irresistible upward surge which had landed us two here.[2]

Such are the noble words of our heroic leader, who not only bore the entire weight of the supreme effort, but also sacrificed his body for the achievement. All of this for the love of the mountains.

We patiently waited for news from Camp IV, hoping that the sahibs would reach the summit. But even so, we could not have imagined the appalling difficulties that would confront them during their perilous descent, and the injuries and harm that would come to them.

On June 5, at dawn, we were all keeping watch when suddenly we thought that we heard faint shouting coming from across the snow slopes. We strained to listen, but the menacing silence that followed filled us with anguish. Mr. Schatz and Mr. Couzy rushed us to climb to Camp V, and we were barely underway when an avalanche swept down the slopes at a dizzying speed, crashing down from the higher camp.

Our blood ran cold as we saw, some distance away, two sahibs half-buried in the snow in a crevasse. Mr. Schatz rushed to them, along with Pansy and me, to help the sahib who was the farthest away and the highest on the glacier. While Pansy and I tended to Mr. Terray, Mr. Schatz helped Bara Sahib, Mr. Lachenal, and Mr. Rébuffat and brought them back down to Camp IV-A. Mr. Schatz returned to the crevasse, risking his life to descend into it and retrieve Bara Sahib's ice axe and camera. Then we began helping Mr. Terray, once again stricken with snow blindness, down the slope. Mr. Lachenal was suffering from serious snow blindness as well, and he followed us, guided by Aïla and Sarki. When everyone met up with Bara Sahib in Camp IV-A, we roped up.

The long, painful, difficult descent began. We crossed a couloir and slopes that were heavily loaded with fresh snow. In the afternoon, while we were descending slowly, a wide, deep crack suddenly opened ahead of us. Bara Sahib tried to climb back up, but Aïla and Sarki were roped to him and pulled him downward. Suddenly all three of them disappeared into the crevasse.

We were thoroughly distraught, but as I was guiding Mr. Terray, who was nearly blind, I could do nothing other than help him to reach the lower camps as safely as possible. I was very worried for the poor sahib who clung desperately to me. I showered him continually with encouragement until we arrived safely in Camp II.

The group came sorrowfully together. We were all horribly affected by the tragedy. But, however dearly it had been paid for, a great victory had just been won: Annapurna had been conquered!

It was a horrifying sight to see Lionel Terray, the great sahib, the *lambawala*, the giant of the group, who had formerly bounded from rock to rock like a tiger, now led by Mr. Schatz at the end of a rope—a fumbling blind man. I could find no words to express what I felt. It was then that I fully understood the spirit that motivated the sahibs, and that was at the heart of their desire to conquer.

Mr. Terray still had that same spirit. He clung to my neck like my own son, although he was taller and broader than I was.

"Everything would be going very well, Ang Tharkay, if I did not have this blasted blindness. But don't worry, things will be better soon."

I knew how much he was suffering: I could feel it in the despair that was etched across his face.

Mr. Ichac came to meet us and walked with us to the camp, where I gently laid Mr. Terray in his bed. The doctor sahib immediately came to take care of him. Then two Sherpas brought Mr. Lachenal on a stretcher. He was in a sad state, snow-blind and with his feet terribly frozen. Bara Sahib was also suffering from serious frostbite.

The fourth sahib who had fallen victim to the snow, Mr. Rébuffat, had frostbitten ears and was completely exhausted. Once the injured were brought into camp, the entire expedition tended to them under the orders of our admirable and tireless doctor. The camp found itself converted into a hospital, the highest-elevation hospital ever.

The doctor sahib had taken command, and his efficient second-in-command was our liaison officer Mr. Noyelle, who organized the return trip down to the smallest detail, with the help of the other sahibs: Mr. Ichac,

Mr. Couzy, and Mr. Schatz. They were constantly shuttling between the bedsides of our four seriously injured men.

I had experienced the greatest mountain epic. I will end my story with the simple and courageous words that our beloved leader, Mr. Maurice Herzog, spoke to me: "We have returned from Annapurna. Lachenal and I reached the summit. My feet and hands are frozen."

| 6 |

THE RETURN

WHILE WE WERE CARING FOR the injured men, I had a great deal of work to do, packing up our supplies and equipment for the return journey. But the doctor sahib was now, without a doubt, the busiest man on the expedition. He went from one patient to another without stopping. We were amazed by the method and science with which he treated the injured sahibs. Our respect and admiration for him grew each day. Thanks to him, little by little, the sahibs' pain was soothed, and the seriousness of their conditions improved.

The critical problem was now to move the injured men down from Camp II to base camp. We had a sled mounted on two skis. The sahibs had used it to go sledding on the snow slopes. As we were not used to this type of vehicle, Mr. Schatz showed us what to do, and he set up the sled on which we had laid Mr. Rébuffat, so that four Sherpas could pull it to Camp I and then down to base camp. As soon as we had left the sahib safely there, we returned for Bara Sahib. After the doctor had examined him again, six of us began pulling his sled down.

I was in charge of the team, and Ichac Sahib came with us. We had to cross several rock bands, and I kept telling my comrades to proceed as gently and cautiously as possible. Three of them held each side of the sled with ropes, and thus we descended the terrifyingly steep rock and ice slopes, creeping under menacing seracs, sinking

into the deep snow, on a journey that was unreal in every way, and at every instant fearing risk of our injured leader's life.

Never had I borne this kind of anxiety. I thanked God and exhaled in relief when we neared Camp I, safe and sound. I stayed there while the sahibs left with Mr. Schatz and Mr. Noyelle to bring Mr. Lachenal down from Camp II. They returned swiftly with their patient, earlier than I ever would have expected. But these two exhausting journeys had left us Sherpas out of breath. We no longer looked energetic, but we were worried about our equipment, which we had left at the higher camps, and we were determined to immediately return to retrieve it. I told Bara Sahib that I was going to climb back to Camp III for the gear, but he became angry, and forbade me and the other Sherpas to hike up to the high camps again. He promised us that he would compensate us handsomely for the loss of our precious possessions.

When I told my companions about Bara Sahib's decision, they seemed satisfied, and their good mood returned for the rest of the journey. The camp was now full, no members of the expedition were missing, and Bara Sahib decided to celebrate our victory.

We all gathered around the tent where Mr. Herzog was. We Sherpas were deeply touched by his generosity at that moment, because he thought to have us all share the single bottle of champagne that remained in the camp. In this way he made all of us part of his victory, and we were just as proud as the sahibs. Never before had we felt such camaraderie and such an intimate bond between the sahibs and ourselves.

But alas, the celebration had barely ended when the doctor inflicted a horrible operation on Bara Sahib. As we listened to his screams of pain, there was not a single one of us Sherpas who was not overwhelmed. We all prayed for him.

At first light the next morning, we rushed to put everything in order for our final march to base camp. The injured sahibs would be carried in a sort of canvas bag that the sahibs called a litter. The sahibs would be seated in it and carried on a man's back. Mr. Lachenal was the first to be carried down like this, accompanied by Mr. Couzy and Mr. Noyelle. On the second trip, we took Rébuffat Sahib, and the next day it was Bara Sahib's turn,

with Adjiba, Sarki, Fou Tharkay, and Pansy carrying him. I was one of the last to go down. Once all of the sahibs had left, I broke down Camp I and accompanied the provisions and equipment that we were bringing down to base camp. I arrived just before nightfall, so exhausted that I immediately fell into a deep sleep.

Our activity was now focused on base camp, where the injured men began receiving more treatment from the indefatigable doctor sahib the next day. I was responsible for transportation, and I was greatly concerned about the porters and coolies. Finding and hiring coolies is like hunting for rare butterflies: always full of the unexpected. As soon as you locate one, it disappears.

Fortunately we had an idea for an irresistible lure. The sahibs had to abandon a large quantity of canned food and tubes of condensed milk to lighten our loads. It was the perfect thing to entice the porters and coolies! I talked to Sarki and a few other comrades, and we distributed the canned food to our potential employees. Our plan was a success: we had all the coolies we needed. As soon as they were hired, we did not waste any time.

The loads were immediately distributed, and we set off for the plains. I waited until all of the sahibs had left before I broke down the camp myself, and then I left with the final loads. We were afraid of being out-run by the monsoon. The rains had already begun, and we were feverishly eager to get on our way. Once the sahibs and the Sherpas who had accompanied them had set off, I left with a group of coolies, and we followed in the others' steps.

Eventually we arrived in a more temperate region, and I lost the feeling in my hands and feet. I forced myself to bring the circulation back by vigorously rubbing them or by walking as fast as I could.

We had to cross a rocky, desert-like spot with no trails at all: nothing but interminable moraine, divided by an infinite expanse of ridges and jumbled rocks, as far as the eye could see. There was not a single level piece of ground: nothing but climbing and going down steep slopes and sharp rocks. When night fell, we felt as if we were lost in a terrifying sea of solitude. We were forced to bivouac for the night in this desert, and our first action was to set up a shelter for Bara Sahib and Mr. Lachenal, who were in such great

need of our care and kindness. Mr. Terray and Mr. Schatz, assisted by Dawa Thondup, never left their bedsides. It was raining torrentially, the cold was bone-chilling, and the wind howled throughout the night. It was impossible to sleep or even to rest at all.

First thing in the morning, we rushed to leave. But there was another major obstacle before us: a river, swollen by the water flowing down from the mountains. We had to cross it to reach the temporary camp that had been set up on the other bank. Mr. Schatz was able to construct a bridge of tree trunks across it, but the coolies were terrified of the water and refused to cross. Adjiba offered, alone, to take Bara Sahib across, and with remarkable skill and a great deal of caution, he succeeded. This example encouraged us all. Finally, through a combination of persuasion and force, we got all of our loads across the river and safely reached the camp.

I had a great deal of trouble with the Tibetan coolies. They stole things from the loads and were always finding reasons to lag behind. I had great difficulty keeping them together, and often I had to resort to force. Once, as we were going down a steep slope, one of them fell behind, and when I found him sitting on a rock, he refused to continue. I forced him to stand up, and I pushed him ahead of me. But as we reached the ridge, he threw his load into the abyss, completely on purpose. I almost pushed him after it, but he was so afraid of my anger that he quickly descended the slope. After an hour of waiting, he came back with his load and continued obediently on his way.

Mr. Terray was now getting better. He nursed Bara Sahib, whose condition—his hands and feet—continued to worsen, and the doctor prepared to amputate fingers and toes. Mr. Terray showed us how to make chairs to carry the wounded men. We then went on a search for trees with flexible branches, and we braided them together to make wicker chairs, one for Bara Sahib and the other for Mr. Lachenal, whose condition was equally serious.

We had to climb back up from 1200 meters to 4500 meters and cross a col that we had traversed on our way to Annapurna. It was brutally cold, and we had no choice but to walk without stopping, in order to keep up our body heat. But because it was late, we had to set up our tents. The only option was a piece of swampy land.

Then we had to descend 1800 meters. The route, across steep, rocky slopes that seemed almost like peaks, appeared terribly dangerous to us. We finally reached the end of the Lete forest, after fording the flood-swollen Chadziou Khola. Because of the precautions we had to take while transporting the injured men, and because of the fluctuations of the current, crossing this river was a feat that each one of us accomplished with a knot of fear in the stomach.

On the path through the Lete forest, there is a little village named Choya. I suggested that we set up our bivouac not far from there, as we could find what we needed for food and water in the village. In addition, the people who lived there were kind and welcoming. But the sahibs were not in the mood to listen to my suggestions. They decided to push on to the Krishna Gandaki, which we crossed on a bridge.[1] We soon arrived at a place where it was decided that we would camp. We stayed for about three days in Lete, and the doctor took advantage of the time to operate on the two sahibs again.

I cannot describe the details of their suffering, especially the pain of our beloved leader. He was the most seriously injured and suffered the amputation of fingers and toes. It is too awful. We all prayed with all our hearts, and, thanks be to God, we had the best doctor that anyone could wish for. These horrifying operations were successful, and although it brought tears to our eyes to see Bara Sahib reduced to this state of extreme weakness, we were truly happy that he was spared from any complications.

One thing that we Sherpas will never forget is the admirable tenderness and brotherly love that the sahibs showed for each other, which did much to hasten the sick men's return to health. When we left Lete, the sahibs were laid on stretchers sent by the official Nepali officer, G. B. Rana, and we left the mountains behind us, finally returning to the plains route.

We were now crossing verdant fields wet with rain. The sun was starting to blaze. The coolies were now exhausted by the heat and caused us a mountain of trouble. The refused to go farther, and a good number of them set down their loads and left us.

We were also suffering from the heat, and we sweated profusely. The sahibs took off their clothes when we stopped to rest, when we could, in

the shade of large trees. Bara Sahib seemed very weak and refused to take any food. Everyone tried to encourage him to eat, but only the doctor sahib succeeded in getting him to take anything. Upon the doctor's orders, Sarki made the sahib eat. I also tried my best, and I cooked a chicken just for him.

"Please, I beg you, eat this," I told him. "You'll see how good it is."

The new coolies that we had hired in Dana seemed to be more worthy than their predecessors and showed that they were very skilled at carrying the sahibs when we continued walking. Sarki had been assigned to watch over Bara Sahib at all times, and I must say that he fulfilled his task remarkably well.

As we approached Beni, we were told that cholera was raging there. We avoided it by crossing the Krishna Gandaki. The bridge looked old and shaky. Adjiba risked it first, carrying Mr. Lachenal, and then he came back for Bara Sahib. I was very worried about transporting our injured this way, when they had suffered so much and their nerves were so raw.

We spent one night in Banduk. It rained torrentially, and then we slowly continued our interminable journey to reach the little village of Kusma. There we had a new crisis with the coolies. Nearly half of our porters had deserted us near Dana, and we did not know how to replace them. I immediately went to see the police *adda* (chief) to ask him to find porters for us. It took nearly two days for him to notify us of the result of his laborious search, which resulted in almost nothing. We had no option other than to break into two groups. I stayed with the second team, along with Adjiba and two sahibs. We were carrying most of the food. We waited two days before continuing on, for better or worse, to rejoin the first team, who were stranded, as more coolies had deserted them.

The small village of Putliket, hidden in the underbrush, is inhabited by a nomadic tribe whose members continually followed us, asking for alms. I grabbed any men I could find, requisitioning them as coolies despite the women's frenetic shouts. The sahibs tried to pacify them with money. But nothing worked: they continued their protestations against us.

I was obliged to force the coolies to continue on with their loads. With our injured sahibs we absolutely could not lose time. So, by conscripting these beggars against their will, we finally reached another village: Garomboree.

We once again began searching for coolies, earning ourselves a reputation as kidnappers or thugs. But when the villagers realized that there was money to be earned, there were more candidates than we wanted. This quest for coolies had become a sport for us throughout our journey.

The monsoon threatened us more and more: we continually heard the roll of thunder, and we suffered through more and more violent rainstorms. At the end of June, we had not yet reached our destination. It was high time that our journey was over. Once we met a man on horseback and stopped him to ask him to find twenty-five coolies for us. The man looked stunned, as if he wondered what we wanted him to do about it. But we were so insistent that we wrestled a promise out of him, but not without holding his horse as a security deposit. We made him walk to the nearest village in order to make sure that he would keep his word. Naturally, he disappeared, and we had to continue on without the coolies but with an extra horse!

While crossing the cornfields, Adjiba, who, with his stocky build and his grumpy disposition, made an ideal recruitment officer, tried to "hire," by will or by force, all of the suitable-looking farmers there. We also called on the services of a Gurkha officer we found there, and the two of them used an infinite variety of tactics to enroll coolies from among the farmworkers. The sahibs succeeded in hiring the Gurkha as an actual recruitment officer, in exchange for ten rupees per day. But he seemed more interested in the money than in his work: we still did not have the required number of coolies. And so we continued, painfully, across the high valleys of Nepal. In Tansing, I met Dawa Thondup, who had left a little before us, and we stayed in the same house for the night.

The next day, we got ahead of the rest of the group. It was a magnificent sunny day, and the heat was crushing. The sahibs were also nervous. I was still looking for coolies. As sirdar, I was responsible for hiring them. Someone from the region truly wanted to help me, and we decided that he would play the role of an army officer and I would be his *subadar*, or adjutant. We went up and down the village streets at a military pace, and we requisitioned porters. The people in the village were so terrified that they scattered every which way, taking refuge in their huts. However, we were able to pin down a couple of recalcitrant villagers whom we were able to bring back to our camp.

When we arrived, I saw a sort of *sadhu* (begging monk) who was trying to pass himself off as a Brahmin. He was muttering prayers and gesturing before Bara Sahib, who was laid out on his stretcher. He was undoubtedly an imposter looking to extort some money from the sahibs. I immediately hired him as a coolie, and I made him carry a load. Along the way, we realized that our sadhu had divested himself of most of his load by dividing it among other coolies. At our first stop, he demanded a salary of four rupees from Bara Sahib. I lost my temper and gave the charlatan a few well-placed kicks. However, to avoid the situation becoming more complicated, I agreed with Bara Sahib to give him two rupees. Let him go to hell!

That happened just before Tansing, a fairly large village that the people in the region generally refer to as Palpa, and where Dawa Thondup and I had spent the night a few days before. The sahibs had not gotten any mail for a long time, and they had sent Ang Tsering (Pansy) to Delhi to retrieve it. They had begun to worry about his absence, when suddenly Pansy appeared with the letters, to the great joy and shouting of the sahibs. They rushed to him and grabbed the packages out of his arms. We were now just on the edge of Tansing, and we began to feel a little more reassured. Now we could glimpse the end of our journey. We were now reentering familiar country. We were finally in a civilized place where the important people came to pay homage to the sahibs and to congratulate them on the expedition's magnificent success.

The governor himself came to visit the sahibs. He brought them the Maharajah's compliments, and he particularly saluted our brave and worthy leader, who was invited to Kathmandu. The people of Tansing treated us as honored guests and gave us an extremely cordial reception. They gave the doctor sahib a tiger skin, and they invited us to a grand reception.

We then rested in Butwal. The doctor sahib treated his patients, which allowed them to undertake their remaining return journey.

Trucks were waiting in Bethari for those of us who were boarding the train at the line's starting point in Nautanwa. I wanted very much to go to Kathmandu before going home, and I was very happy to be invited by Bara Sahib to accompany him there. When we arrived in Raxaul that night, I went with two companions to a hotel and learned the very alarming news

that there had been a serious landslide in Darjeeling. Then I could think only of returning home as soon as possible.

The restaurant owner gave me a horrifying description of the cataclysm. He told me that nearly six hundred people had perished. Worse, he specified that the neighborhood of Bhotey Butsy, where I lived, had been particularly hard hit. My throat tightened, and I hastily returned to see the sahibs to tell them that I was abandoning the idea of going to Kathmandu. I asked Bara Sahib for permission to return home immediately. After a sad goodbye to the great leader and the other brave sahibs, I set off alone for Siliguri and Darjeeling. I arrived a little after midnight in Siliguri, but no one there could give me any details on what had happened in Darjeeling.

I could not sleep all night, as I waited impatiently for the morning train to take me to Darjeeling. When I arrived, I asked the first person I saw about what had happened. She was a woman I knew. She reassured me and told me that my loved ones were completely fine but that they had barely escaped. When the landslide had threatened our house, our friends had gotten together and come to help my wife and children evacuate the dangerous area and move to safer quarters.

I was soon reunited—with such happiness!—with my wife and children.

| 7 |

A WEEK IN PARIS

DURING THE FIRST WEEK OF March 1953, I received a kind invitation from Mr. Herzog to travel to Paris for the showing of the film *Victory on Annapurna*, which was scheduled for April 2. I was very touched and carried away with joy. Going to Europe on an airplane went beyond anything a Sherpa could aspire to.

I lost control of myself. I imagined everything that this journey might hold, this marvelous trip to the country that the sahibs came from. The news spread quickly in Darjeeling, and I was soon besieged with visitors. Some of them advised me not to risk angering the gods again by agreeing to go to the land of the "white men," after having desecrated the gods' home at the summit of Annapurna. But most of my Sherpa colleagues and my close friends congratulated me with no afterthoughts. They envied the privilege that I enjoyed and the honor bestowed upon me.

I had no time to lose. As I had never been outside my home country, I was totally ignorant about the administrative formalities and rules that have to be complied with when one wants to go abroad. The secretary of the Darjeeling Himalayan Club was kind enough to give me a letter for his colleague in the Calcutta section, and armed with the two hundred rupees that Mr. Herzog had generously sent me, I left for Calcutta on the plane. It was my first experience of an airplane flight, and I was extremely happy during this brief trip. As

soon as I arrived at the Himalayan Club, the secretary brought me to the French consulate. Things moved quickly. In less than forty-eight hours, the consulate did what was needed for my passport and for the visas. On March 30, I was ready to leave for France via Karachi.

We took off from Dum Dum, the Calcutta airport, at one o'clock in the afternoon, and we reached Karachi at five o'clock the next day. After stopping for a few hours we took off again, and we arrived in Rome via Beirut at eight o'clock that night. Flying over the Alps reminded me of our gigantic Himalayan summits. The Alps were bluer and more separated, and the magnificent landscape around them served as the perfect backdrop. It was not surprising that the European climbers held their mountains in such high regard, even when they threw themselves into Himalayan expeditions. I also would have liked to climb these magnificent peaks that rose up before my eyes.

From Beirut to Rome, we followed the Mediterranean coast. For me, this was a completely new sight, intensely green and a stark contrast with the arid and sandy countries of the Middle East. We were so high in the air that I could barely make out the ports on the Italian coast, with the ships like tiny moving dots in the sea, and trains on the land. The green hills that hemmed in the shoreline brought me peace and comfort. I felt an indefinable sense of exile when we neared this strange and marvelous country, where the masters of the world tend to live. I felt completely inferior to the white sahibs whom I had served for many years during their Himalayan expeditions.

I finally arrived at Paris-Orly on April 1, 1953, at two o'clock in the morning. The flight attendant asked me to wait in the airplane until all of the other passengers had disembarked, and this odd request greatly distressed me. Maybe, I told myself, they were suspicious of me, which would have embarrassed me more because I could neither ask questions nor understand what was being explained to me. I did not know more than one or two words of French or English, and nothing of any other European language, and I certainly did not expect that anyone would understand Nepali or Hindi. So there was nothing to do but remain seated and wait silently and anxiously.

Suddenly I was led out of the airplane. Before I could gather my thoughts, I found myself before a phalanx of filmmakers, and their flashbulbs exploded

in my face. I was blinded and disoriented. I felt reassured only when I fell into the arms of my dear old friend Marcel Ichac, who pushed me into the arms of another longtime acquaintance, one of my countrymen, L. S. Bangdel. No doubt Mr. Ichac did this to show me that I would not be left alone in an unknown country, and that I was assured of being in the company of a man from my own country. In fact I would be reunited with other friends: my dear sahibs. They were all going to be there to welcome me to the illustrious and magnificent country. Marcel Ichac insisted on carrying my suitcase, with these simple words that I will never forget: "Ang Tharkay, in the Himalaya you were our porter, but today I will be yours."

From the airport, I was taken to the hotel, where a luxury apartment had been reserved for me, for my entire stay in Paris. All of this made me feel as if I were in a dream, and I marveled at the cards that destiny had dealt me, plunging me, a poor little Sherpa from an impoverished country, lost in the shadows of the Himalayas, into this kind of luxury.

I was in a state of shock. I was incapable of sleeping for the rest of the night. I sat awake in my bed, asking myself a thousand questions about what was going to happen.

Around nine o'clock, Bangdel came to see how I was doing and to give me the pleasure of keeping me company during breakfast. Bangdel's deep knowledge of Paris began to reassure me, and I felt a bit less out of my element. Little by little I shed my fear and let the spirit of Paris infuse me.

That same morning at around ten o'clock, Mr. Schatz and Mr. Ichac came to take me to a stylish Parisian tailor. They wanted to dress me like a Frenchman, in a suit, a dress shirt, socks, and shoes in the latest fashion. In sum, they wanted to transform me into a true Parisian for a few days.

I felt as if I were being costumed for a parade, and I amused myself by thinking of what my Sherpa countrymen would have said if they had seen me.

Bangdel had a truly Asian sense of cleverness, and he greeted me in the Sherpa way when he saw me emerge, fully Europeanized from head to toe and ready to get into the car that had been kindly provided to me to tour Paris. I was speechless as we drove silently through the streets and boulevards as smooth as mirrors, or along avenues lined with magnificent trees,

while we passed before the marvelous palaces of emperors and kings, and along the lawns decorated with exquisitely graceful fountains. The order and harmony of the streets and public spaces for these incredibly charming and civil people will be forever etched in my memory.

The moment had arrived for a meeting that was extremely important to me: with Maurice Herzog, our beloved Bara Sahib, who was returning from New York that very afternoon. We rushed to Orly to meet him.

What a joyful reunion! There are no words to describe what we both felt when we met again. I welcomed him with the warmth of the deep and very respectful affection that I had always felt for him. When we met, we immediately relived the memories of our common struggle, and of the highs and lows of our adventure on Annapurna. Alas! All that I could find to say, stammering and full of confusion, was: "Bara Sahib, I am very happy to see you!"

Shortly after three o'clock, we left for the French Alpine Club, where a grand reception was given in honor of the expedition members. There were crowds of men and women in the salons. The president of the Alpine Club awarded me a gold medal. I have never felt so intimidated, so confused by my ignorance, as I did there in the middle of this distinguished assembly. I clung desperately to Bangdel, as he was the only one I could count on. I remember that he tried to get me to say a few words in Hindi into the microphone, but my mouth was paralyzed and I could not say even a single word. The French were too generous and understanding to insist. They did not even give me enough time to be ashamed of my embarrassment. There was always someone close by who put me at ease. Oh, how I wished I knew a few words in their language to tell all my French friends how grateful and happy I was. May God bless them!

From the Alpine Club, we went to the Marignan cinema, where the film that Marcel Ichac had made about Annapurna was being shown to a select audience: ministers, members of the diplomatic corps (including the Indian ambassador), Sirdar Malik, and many members of Parisian high society. A place of honor had been reserved for me among this elite, next to the expedition chief Maurice Herzog himself. I was terribly confused by these honors. For me, it was an unforgettable evening. Everyone wanted to talk to me,

even the Indian ambassador who took me aside and spoke to me alone for a few minutes.

What an unbelievable sight to see our adventure on Annapurna on the screen! The film was a perfect retelling of our expedition. I was absolutely enchanted by it, and through it I relived all of the events and dangers that we had survived. Now that I could see all of it through Marcel Ichac's camera as I sat in an armchair, I was very happy that the experience was over!

Over the next few days, I visited tourist attractions and was invited by my hosts' families to their homes. Unfortunately, the visits were so rushed that I was not able to keep a lasting impression of any particular place, with the exception of an excursion to the Fontainebleau forest organized by Mr. Lucien Devies, the president of the French Mountain Federation. I was enchanted by this forest, because, with its rounded rocks and cool, shady valleys, it reminded me of my homeland in Solu-Khumbu. I was surprised to find many people there, both men and women, who were playing at mountaineering with miniature camps and mountaineering clothing and equipment. They seemed just as passionate as we were about our expeditions. The sahibs and their wives begged me to do a rock-climbing demonstration on the slippery rocks, even offering to lend me their shoes for the occasion. I spent very happy times in the company of these charming people who did not know how much pleasure they brought me.

After that, I was taken to a restaurant and treated to a sumptuous meal, accompanied by as many different wines as I wanted. It goes without saying that I consumed as much as I could.

I had to say a few words into the national radio station's microphone. Bangdel had prepared a little speech for me, and then he translated it into English. That was the first time that I had heard my voice on tape, and I couldn't even recognize it. I even doubted that what I had said to Bangdel was reproduced exactly.

I could not get used to wearing a necktie in the French style. It was a combination of a collar and a knot of fabric, so often I would go down to the lobby of my hotel having forgotten to put on my tie.

Marcel Ichac did not give me a moment's rest, as he was committed to showing me every element of *la grande vie* in Paris. I could not miss the

Folies-Bergère. There is certainly no other place in the world that can compare to it. What I saw there made me think of the *Thousand and One Nights* stories that I had been told. When I later described certain scenes in the show to my Sherpa countrymen, they could do nothing but laugh incredulously, as if these were fairy tales or stories that I had invented. Bangdel explained to me that Paris is the capital city of pleasure, and the Folies-Bergère is its temple. I too was intoxicated by the seductive spectacle.

No one can visit Paris without taking a ride on its extraordinary Metro, an underground train system that transports residents back and forth across the capital, comfortably and on time.

And now for the Eiffel Tower! This was the climax of my stay in the world's most stunning city. It was there that we celebrated our Annapurna campaign during an intimate gathering. Bara Sahib, Maurice Herzog, had organized this event himself, with all the love and graciousness that reign over a family reunion. Nearly all the expedition members along with their wives and loved ones were there. Maurice Herzog's mother embraced me as if I was her own son, and this touched me deeply. Mrs. Ichac gave me all sorts of delicious Parisian sweets for my children.

This leads me to discuss the marvels of French cuisine. The French have food and drinks of an unbelievable deliciousness and beauty. Unfortunately I cannot remember the names, nor can I pronounce them, so my countrymen must withstand their curiosity. At the Eiffel Tower restaurant, a truly royal meal was prepared for me, a sort of "gala tiffin." All of my friends signed the menu from that day, and I kept it as a souvenir of this unforgettable reunion. We were served an extraordinary cake named Annapurna. I have never since seen or tasted anything like it, and I cannot even begin to explain how it was made or how divine it was. Oh, these French "chefs"! What a meal, what a table, and what company! I still think about it with a sharp pang of nostalgia.

We met at the Alpine Club in the evenings. There Bara Sahib gave me a superb watch as a gift. I was also given a gold chain as well as bracelets for my wife. He was the kindest and most generous person toward me. When the departure day finally came, my heart was torn between two feelings: the desire to see my little house in Darjeeling again and my newly discovered love of Paris.

I am very grateful for all the goodwill that Mr. Lucien Devies, the president of the French Mountain Federation, showed me. He took care of me during the last two days that I spent in the French capital. Neither will I ever forget my old friend Bangdel, who remained constantly by my side as a precious companion and helper. Without his kindness and help, I would have felt lost in Paris.

Mr. Devies and Bangdel accompanied me to Orly, where I had to catch the airplane that would take me home. I felt such a deep sadness when it came time to leave Paris that I decided to drink in order to drown my sorrows, before I was buckled into my seat. I remember having told Bangdel that not until I had returned to reality, at the foot of the Himalaya, would I truly understand the magnificent dream that I had just experienced. This extraordinary week remains unforgettable for me. It is my comfort. I think of it every time I am sad.

EPILOGUE: NUN KUN

DURING MY VISIT TO PARIS, Mr. Bernard Pierre and I had agreed that I would accompany him to Nun Kun, a relatively unknown massif in the western Himalayas. The highest summit, the 7135 meter Nun, was still unclimbed. We were scheduled to set off in the middle of July 1953. New Delhi was our meeting point. The expedition included two Indian officers, four sahibs, a memsahib, and six Sherpas.[1]

After we had obtained our entry permit for Kashmir, we left New Delhi by train on July 11, headed for Pathankot. From there we went to Jammu by car. The soldiers stationed in Jammu helped us cross the flood-swollen rivers, and thus we arrived at the Udhampur camp.

The next day, we left for Doda, a village in the northwest of the district of Jammu, on the Kashmir border. We had decided to stop there for two days to organize the approach march. In Doda, the Swiss missionary pastor Pierre Vittoz, whom Mr. Bernard Pierre had invited to join the expedition, came to find us. All of us Sherpas were thoroughly surprised to hear one of the sahibs speak our language. The pastor lived in Ladakh, on the India–Tibet border. We left Doda on July 15, with the sahibs continuing on by jeep for twenty-three kilometers, while we followed along with a mule train. Thus we covered the forty-three kilometers that separated us from Thatri, the end of our first stage.

When we arrived at the village in the middle of the night, we went to stay in a government bungalow. Then we set off for Kishtwar, a fairly large town,

where we decided to stay for two days as well. That gave us enough time to purchase food and fuel. When we arrived, all of the residents gathered around. They seemed suspicious of us, maybe thinking that we intended to kidnap their children. At first their attitude was hostile, but little by little they became more cordial as they saw how foolish their worries were.

We left Kishtwar on July 18. The next day we arrived in Ikhale, and we would leave there the following morning for another village, Lopara, where we were to spend the night. The next stop was Hanzale, from where we would reach Napachi, the largest village that we had encountered. We stayed there for three days. We decided that from there on we would not use pack mules, and instead we would hire coolies. We also had to restock our food and fuel for the rest of the trip. Hiring coolies was an even more delicate issue than usual, and the bara sahib (Pierre) had to negotiate for an entire afternoon in order for them to agree to a decent price, since their demands were highly exaggerated.[2]

On July 25 we reached the mountainous region. In Tashparu, we were provided with the government bungalow reserved for civil servants from the Topographic Service, but it was very dilapidated, having not been used for years. We learned that it had been occupied, long before we arrived, by Japanese explorers hunting for herbs and medicinal plants that flourished in the region.

We had arrived at the confluence of two rivers, the Zaz Nal and the Rin Nal. We had to cross one of them on an improvised bridge, then, from the other bank, we had to climb a rocky promontory. We were already at more than 3000 meters. Wood was becoming scarce, and the coolies announced that they refused to go farther. Through persuasion, the bara sahib and I succeeded in convincing them to stay with us.

During the entire approach march, the memsahib had surprised us with her agility and endurance. She always walked first, shaming us with unflagging bravery and energy, even when her feet were ravaged with bleeding blisters. Base camp was—finally—established on July 30 at an altitude of 4700 meters, at the south face of Nun. Two days later, the bara sahib and the pastor sahib took me to choose the location for Camp I and immediately establish it at 5400 meters. When this work was done, we climbed with the

bara sahib, Michel Sahib (Michel Desorbay), and the doctor sahib to 5850 meters to establish Camp II.[3] In the fog we had a great deal of difficulty finding a suitable location. Finally we found a small plateau that hung over an icefall. We thought that it would be just big enough to set up our tents. Unfortunately the next day we were unable to establish Camp III, as the monsoon was threatening. We first had to descend to Camp I, then finally to base camp, where we waited for a week for the weather to improve. On August 19, the bara sahib decided to set off again. The next day we arrived at Camp II. From there, we made a route to Camp III at 6420 meters where, alas, we were immobilized for two days by a formidable snowfall. It fell so thickly that it was impossible for us to try to reach the summit.

On August 23, the bara sahib once again had to state his decision to descend. He asked me to take the lead on the rope that included himself, Michel Desorbay, and me. The pastor sahib, the memsahib, and the doctor sahib followed behind.

Suddenly, a few hundred meters from Camp II, we heard a horrible cracking sound and the thick rumbling of snow and ice crashing down on us. The avalanche had released one hundred meters above us and came directly down on our group. In the blink of an eye, we were caught. All three of us were knocked down and rolled over each other. Luckily, we had fallen into deep snow. The pastor sahib's rope was able to stop their slide very quickly. But our rope was carried off in a hellish, swirling vortex for many hundreds of meters. In the meantime, the other group had descended to help us. Our situation appeared tragic: Michel Desorbay had completely disappeared under the snow. Only his hand was visible. With the help of one of the sahibs, I was able to free his head. His mouth was packed with snow. The bara sahib and I were also in an unfortunate state.[4] We were immediately transported to Camp II. There the doctor sahib examined us and treated us with great care and attention. After taking medications and withstanding some injections, we were able to reach Camp I, then base camp. We stayed there for two days, and the expedition regrouped for one final attempt.

The bara sahib decided to form two new assault teams. The first, composed of the memsahib, the pastor sahib, and himself, left on the first day. Their goal was Camp III. The second group, composed of the doctor sahib

and Michel Sahib, set off the next day for Camp I. I stayed at base camp with Kami Sherpa, whose lungs were congested.[5]

When the first group arrived at the location of Camp III, the camp was no longer there. There was no trace of it! Fortunately the climbers had brought a tent and a bit of food from Camp II. But they had no stove. For drinking water they had to melt snow over a candle flame. Pemba Norbu Sherpa spent the night with them. The three other Sherpas descended to Camp II. Despite these precarious conditions and the bitterly cold weather, the sahibs were determined to launch the final assault on the morning of August 28.

Fortunately the storm cleared and the weather was very good. Bara Sahib had to admit that he was no longer in any condition to continue, after his recent accident and the injuries that he had suffered. He had already expended a great deal of energy to accompany his comrades to that point, and the Sherpas had admired his tenacity. Bara Sahib understood that he was too slow. He would hold the pastor sahib and the memsahib back, and he might compromise their success in the end. So, midway to the summit, he turned around and returned to Camp III with Pemba Norbu. The lady and the pastor were solid as a Himalayan rock as they continued on alone and reached the 7135-meter summit of Nun, at about four o'clock.

During that time, I waited at base camp for their return. The day after their victory, the two groups met there, and we celebrated the event. We were all the more enthusiastic because of our great effort and the great dangers we had confronted. All of the Sherpas applauded the memsahib. We considered her a great heroine. We were surprised by her remarkable abilities as a mountaineer.

But this success had been earned narrowly before the rains came. Already the monsoon was breaking, and a fierce lightning storm gave the signal to the heavenly bodies. Under a torrential rain the expedition set off on the return route through the valley. We had barely left base camp when the deluge unleashed its fury on us. We were soaked to the bone when we reached our first stop: a dilapidated nomads' hut with a sieve-like roof. The coolies were exhausted, and the next day one of them lay down in despair, in the middle of the trail. The cold and dampness had completely numbed his legs.

But we had to continue walking to reach Tashparu as soon as possible. The coolies lagged behind, endlessly stopping to take shelter from the rain under the rock overhangs that we passed. Bara Sahib and I wasted a great deal of time goading them along. We were far behind the main group, and I wondered if we would ever reach our destination that night. We were soaked, exhausted, and at our wits' end. Finally we arrived in Tashparu.

From there we set off again for Napachi and stayed there to rest for two days, which we desperately needed. From Napachi we reached Srinagar after many stages. That was the end of the expedition, and there our dear bara sahib gave a great party for everyone. He invited many additional people. It was a worthy celebration of our victory on Nun. At that dinner, I met again a woman I knew as Helen Memsahib, a longtime friend and protector of Sherpas.[6] She gave me an affectionate tribute and a heap of gifts for my family and me. It had been fourteen years since I had seen her, and I was touched that she still remembered my comrades and me. She was a true friend to us.

We stayed in Srinagar for three days, and from there we left to return home to Darjeeling. Mr. Bernard Pierre, the memsahib (Claude Kogan), Helen Memsahib, and the other sahibs came to say goodbye to us. Touching, marked by sadness and affection, these were farewells among friends.

The Nun Kun expedition was my last as a sirdar. It remains one of my best and most passionate memories, out of all of the expeditions that I took part in.

After my trip to Paris, I was happy to return to mountaineering with my French friends, on an adventure in which courage and friendship were such a beautiful part.

I am more than satisfied to end this modest tale on that thought. May it serve as the grateful tribute that I offer to all those who allowed me to live ever after with the exalted memory of the joys and pain that I experienced alongside them.

PRAISE AND TESTIMONIALS

I AM NOT A POET. I make no claims as an artist. But I have a sensitive heart and a faithful memory. I am capable of deeply loving living beings and things. Within this love, there is a happiness that neither words nor images can express, and I have taken great pleasure in remembering all of the close friendships that circumstances have brought me.

During one of our expeditions, we were followed by a Tibetan dog. He quickly worked his way into our group and always stood guard outside the camp kitchen. As I was normally in charge of the meals, he followed me everywhere. He had developed an unyielding attachment to me, and soon became my bodyguard.

At night he slept in front of the door to my tent, no matter how brutal the temperature was. He was my gentle, affectionate, and faithful companion. I was the only thing that mattered to him, which was sometimes very embarrassing. He quickly became accustomed to my routines and my personality. He never left my side, even when I left the kitchen to climb steep snow slopes. He recognized my name and pricked up his ears when he heard it, and he would look at me to see my reaction.

People ended up thinking of him as "Ang Tharkay's shadow." No one else liked him. He hindered my relationships with other people, and I felt that he provoked hostility in my comrades. He was an enormous, ferocious-looking beast, but with me he was as sweet as a lamb and always ready to obey the smallest command from me.

One day, while we were coming back from a high camp, Togo, as we called him, was docilely following me down a steep slope covered with a thick layer of snow. I was roped up with two other Sherpas, and I went first. I was so careful to leave a trail and so worried about avoiding the threat of avalanches that I totally forgot about Togo. The snow fell hard, and we hurried to base camp. All of a sudden my crampons slipped, and I started sliding. I pulled my two companions down with me, but my arm was inexplicably held fast by something firm and unshakable. Thanks to that support I was able to get back on my feet, and with shock and gratitude I found that Togo had saved me by holding on to my bag with the fiercest possible determination. I looked around me and saw my two comrades buried in the snow. I quickly pulled them out. We barely had the time to shake the snow off when we had to descend as fast as possible, hearing the rumble, louder and louder, of an avalanche that was rolling toward us. Luck allowed us to escape to safety. We were happy and relieved to have escaped that danger, but not for an instant did we think of the brave and faithful dog that had sacrificed himself to save us. Alas, the avalanche had swallowed poor Togo just after he had saved us. He was buried at the very spot where I had fallen. The avalanche must have surprised him before he could run away. For the rest of my life I will remember this faithful friend with regret. He was true and devoted, and gave his life for me.

Aside from this wordless friendship, I have countless memories of my friendships, large and small, with Himalayan mountaineers. They left me with profound memories, and I want to say a few words about them.

First I must mention Mr. Eric Shipton, the great pioneer of Everest expeditions. His renowned reconnaissance expedition in 1951 was, as I have said, the prelude to the conquest that would happen two years later. For me, our collaboration was memorable, and every time that I want to rekindle my fervent attachment to this leader, I repeat these lines that he wrote in my autograph book:

> *I have known Ang Tharkay for many years. As soon as we met, I felt*
> *a deep admiration for him, and on every expedition, my affection*
> *for him only grew. It is not just the servant in him that I appreciate,*

but the friend and companion who takes his fair share of the action, without ever abusing the confidence placed in him.

What he has done speaks volumes about him. I have known him since the 1933 expedition to Everest. He climbed to Camp IV (7830 meters). He was part of the group that was stranded there for three days during a snowstorm. Most of the other porters suffered from frostbite or were too exhausted to continue climbing above the North col. Only two men did this, and Ang Tharkay was one of them. This time he reached Camp V (8347 meters).

In 1934, he was with Tilman and myself when we entered the Nanda Devi basin, and during our two explorations of the sources of the Ganges. He showed himself to be incredibly resourceful, persever- ant and a skilled mountaineer. Although our expedition lasted five months, he was heavy-hearted when we began the return journey.

In 1935, he joined our Everest reconnaissance, where he showed great skill as an instructor. He was once again with us on Everest in 1936; although he had been promoted to sirdar, he carried a load as usual. In the fall of that same year, he accompanied Osmaston and myself on our exploration of the Nanda Devi basin.

In 1937, I had placed him in charge of hiring my Sherpas for the Shaksgam expedition; it was a difficult task. He showed admirable judgment. During that expedition, he frequently had to lead a rope, or do a reconnaissance of an itinerary, or sort loads. More than once, he and the other Sherpas carried up to sixty kilos over difficult terrain.

Once, while we were roped together, he pulled me out of a crevasse into which I had fallen, and where I hung by the rope.

In 1938, Mrs. Odling very kindly took him to her home for several months so that he could learn to cook for the Everest expedition.

*During this expedition, he was our cook and performed his task per-
fectly. He still carried the same load as everyone else, and once again
that year he climbed to over 8,200 meters.*

*In 1939, the year when I am writing this, he accompanied me
to the Karakoram. The expedition was meant to last eighteen
months, but because of the war, we called it off at the end of the
summer campaign.*

*Ang Tharkay proved equal to what he had always been, and I con-
tinue to hold him as the best Sherpa I have ever known.*

To these words I will add a few other testimonials. I will cite them here, not
to enumerate the qualities that they ascribe to me, but so that they can serve
as an honorable record of these everlasting friendships and as a testimony to
this powerful link that unites everyone who is passionate about Himalayan
adventuring.

*After the tribute that Shipton has just written for Ang Tharkay,
what else can I say at the end of a brief journey into the mountains,
other than this: if there is a man who is always joyful, hardworking
and open-minded, Ang Tharkay is surely that man.*

R. S. Cranston (November 27, 1943)

*I have just concluded a journey to Phalut and Panmyonché with
Ang Tharkay as sirdar and cook. He proved himself to be dedicated,
capable and full of good humor. For me, it was a revelation to dis-
cover the extent to which an expedition under his leadership can be
pleasant and trouble-free.*

Geo E. Kempe

*Ang Tharkay was our sirdar and cook during a brief voyage to
Gyantse, Tibet. He is indisputably the best Sherpa I have ever met;
although this time he did not have the chance to climb very high [or]*

show his skill as a climber. He is a good cook and knows how to vary the meals. His organization of the transportation and the manner in which he handled the coolies' work proved to be excellent. They were always calculated exactly. His knowledge of the Tibetans and their language was invaluable. Without him, the difficulties that we encountered and the costs of our trip would have been much greater.

F. S. Smythe, R.A.F.

The Sherpa Ang Tharkay is a very old friend of mine. He accompanied me on many trips to Sikkim, including the expedition to Kabru in 1935. He also accompanied us, D. H. McPherson and I, during a month (October to November) in 1944, and his presence greatly enhanced the enjoyment of that trip, although because of the poor weather, we were not able to complete our planned climbs. Ang Tharkay once more proved his skill and strength when it came to carrying loads over difficult snow slopes. It was he who cooked our food throughout the journey, and he knew how to make the most of the meager resources that we had in Sikkim during the war.

During the first three years of the war, he worked as a porter for me, although expeditions were almost impossible, and I am impatiently waiting for the day when rationing and the other difficulties will end, allowing him to leave his family in Darjeeling and join a team with me again. Unless, of course, his services are required for more important undertakings such as a new Everest expedition.

Lt. Col. C. R. Cooke (November 14, 1944)

In 1947, that same Lieutenant Colonel Cooke wrote:

I want to say once more that Ang Tharkay accompanied G. Schoberth and me in November 1935, as our primary high-altitude porter during a very brief five-week expedition, the primary outcome of which was the ascension of the north peak of Kabru, and the summit of Dome [Dome Ridge Peak].

In 1948, D.F. Wood told the story of our first meeting:

> *That was the first time that I met Ang Tharkay. I was immediately*
> *struck not only by his strength and vigor, which of course are well*
> *known, but also by his youthful enthusiasm for mountaineering (a*
> *character trait that, I am pleased to say, he never lost). For our little*
> *group, he was a precious discovery.*
>
> *Ang Tharkay served as my sirdar during a three-week journey that*
> *I took to the Donkga-La. He had chosen five excellent Sherpas in*
> *Darjeeling, and he managed them perfectly. He also was respon-*
> *sible for the cooking, and personally served me. His talents in that*
> *area are remarkable. The meals that he prepared for us at 5,500*
> *meters, made in blustering wind under the most precarious condi-*
> *tions, would shame the meals in many hotels. During an assault, he*
> *was my rope-mate and showed a very good sense for the mountain.*
> *Above all, I will never forget his unflagging good humor and his*
> *obvious popularity among the porters. I surely hope to have a chance*
> *to call on his services again.*
>
> <div align="right">D. F. Wood (October 30, 1948)</div>

And in 1949, Mr. Wood wrote:

> *Ang Tharkay again accompanied me this year on a three and a*
> *half-week journey that I took to Lhonak. He took care of all the*
> *organization, including the porters and the rations, and he always*
> *prepared excellent meals for me. He guided our group from the high*
> *camp to the Jonsong La; without him I would undoubtedly not*
> *have reached it, as I was not acclimatized nor was I in a condition*
> *to direct the climb. During this climb, his energy and good humor*
> *never waned, as is always true of him. He showed himself to be*
> *resourceful and very thrifty when it came to purchasing things*
> *along the way.*

Here are a few lines from the Himalayan climber Trevor Braham:

I think that I was very lucky to have Ang Tharkay as a sirdar during a one-month journey that I took to Sikkim this year. I have nothing to add to everything that has already been said about him. I can only confirm that he is an exceptional Sherpa and a charming travel companion. The way in which he organizes the colleagues he has selected and gets them to hike is unique. He often uses his sense of humor and playfulness, and the results are undeniable. We can count on him in any situation. There is no difficulty, no matter how large, that he cannot resolve, and he avoids anything that is not related to the expedition's goal. It is surely thanks to his great knowledge of the mountains and his judgment that it was possible for me to undertake a study of a glacier that had never been explored, and to find a way off this glacier via an unknown col, at 5,800 meters. An attempt on Kanchenjunga failed at 6,400 meters, due to the cold and violent wind, although the terrain was not difficult and the snow conditions were satisfactory. Ang Tharkay was the only Sherpa who recoiled at the idea of abandoning this attempt, and despite the danger of frostbite, I was almost ashamed at having given the order to retreat.

As far as his talents in the kitchen, I will say only this: during the entire month, I did not lack one single time for fresh meat, vegetables, fruits, eggs and the sophisticated meals that he prepared under the most difficult circumstances; they were often mind-blowing. Somehow, mysteriously, he always found a way to anticipate what we wanted, and when we wanted it.

I can say in all sincerity that the success of this expedition and the pleasure that I took in it are largely due to him, and I have no desire to return to these mountains unless he accompanies me.

Trevor Braham (November 21, 1949)

Finally, from Mr. Bernard Pierre:

Ang Tharkay was the sirdar for our expedition to Nun Kun (July, August, September 1953).

It is difficult to sing the praises of a sirdar who has such a magnificent roll of accomplishments, and who is universally praised. Nevertheless I would like to say how much I appreciated his integrity, his devotion, his spirit of initiative, and his unequaled sense of the mountain.

Ang Tharkay takes true joy in conquering a Himalayan summit.

For us, he was a true friend. And that is how we thought of him.

Afterword by Dawa Sherpa

When my father, Ang Tharkay, was a young man, his father's close friend, a shaman from a Rai family, told him to run away from his village so he could have a better life in the future—that if he stayed in the village, he would only have poverty. That is why he ran away to Darjeeling where he met my mother and started working for climbing expeditions. He tells the story of some of those expeditions in this book.

In 1954 Ang Tharkay became an instructor at the newly opened Himalayan Institute of Mountaineering. After a few years of working with road-building crews in Sikkim, he was asked to be sirdar for the 1960 Indian Everest Expedition, led by Captain Kohli. He was happy to be back in the Himalayas and to meet his old friends and relatives. Things had not changed much in his village, but he found that many Sherpas were now participating in expeditions.

Because he never liked living in cities, in about 1968 my father bought a piece of barren land ninety kilometers south of Kathmandu near Daman, the small village where you encounter the first, and highest, hills when you approach from the south. For me it was a gateway to the Himalayas. My father first built a house, then a farm on that land with rocks all around. Initially he partnered with some friends, and the farm had cows and pigs, but the pigs were a problem. As a Buddhist my father could not kill the animals to be sold for meat. His friends left the farm, and my father continued the farm on his own, with forty cows. He loved animals, and he was concerned

about the environment. He never used any chemical products on the farm. He cared about others as well. He brought some homeless families from Darjeeling to live on the land that he farmed.

My father was a simple and a very hardworking person, always with a smile on his face. Every morning he would go through his Pechas, the holy Tibetan Buddhist books. That is how he started his day, every day. Within our family, he did not talk much about the mountains and the expeditions he had gone on, but we learned about his expeditions when he talked about them to others. He was a very peaceful person, and I never heard him insult or criticize anyone. He did not like political parties, and he particularly disliked the communists because the Chinese communists had destroyed the *gompas* (monasteries) in Tibet.

Some years after my father died, there was a big landslide, and the house, as well as some of the land, was swept away. Our family then gave part of the surviving property to the Tibetan lamas for a small monastery. We also gave some land for a school that JAITI (Japanese Agricultural In-Service Training Institute) was building. Until then there had been no school for the poor children of the village. On the top of the hill of the farm, my eldest brother, Mr. Lobsang Tenzing Sherpa, started a garden of rhododendrons from all over the region. He has passed away, but we continue his efforts, hoping that future generations will always enjoy the beauty of this region, the gateway of the Himalayas.

My father used to tell us, "You must go to school to get an education for a better job and for a better life. Forget about going to the mountains as a Sherpa on expeditions. Life as a Sherpa is not a joke. It is real hard and you would not earn a good salary." Today I feel I've been a very lucky person to have had such a father.

ACKNOWLEDGMENTS

FOR THE ORIGINAL EDITION (1954)

The editors are profoundly grateful to the Austrian expert ethnologist, Mr. C. von Fürer Haimendorf, a member of the School of Oriental and African Studies at the University of London. He was kind enough to read the first few chapters of Ang Tharkay's book and filled in numerous details.

At present, Mr. C. von Fürer Haimendorf is the only expert who has conducted a serious ethnographic study in the land of the Sherpas, during his recent extended stay there.

PUBLISHER'S NOTE (2016)

This first-ever English-language edition would not exist were it not for the actions of a great many individuals, several of whom we would like to thank here. Bill Petroske not only brought *Memoires d'un Sherpa* to our attention but also provided a copy of the very rare French-language edition, with no guarantee that anything would come of his generosity. Several of our Legends and Lore advisors were invaluable in locating Ang Tharkay's son, Dawa Sherpa, who so kindly provided the new afterword for this edition. Tashi Sherpa both encouraged us to publish his uncle's story and also agreed without hesitation to write the new foreword. Bill Buxton and Bob A. Schelfhout Aubertijn devoted countless hours to fact-checking the text

and writing the majority of the new footnotes. The two also researched and compiled the Expedition History Summary and the extensive new bibliography. The depth and breadth of their knowledge and their dedication are truly staggering. Finally, we thank Ang Tharkay himself for being so inspirational a figure—without him, it is clear, many of our favorite mountaineering adventures might never have been written.

—Mountaineers Books

EXPEDITION HISTORY SUMMARY

Date	Destination	Expedition leader(s)	Role	Account	Notes
1931	Kanchenjunga	Paul Bauer	Porter	Bauer's *Kanchenjunga Challenge*	Ang Tharkay's first expedition
1933	Everest (North)	Hugh Ruttledge		Ruttledge's *Everest 1933*	
1934	Nanda Devi Sanctuary	Eric Shipton and Bill Tilman	Sirdar	Shipton's *Nanda Devi*	Ang Tharkay was formally made sirdar for first time.
1935	Everest (North) Reconnaissance	Eric Shipton	Sirdar	Shipton's *The Mount Everest Reconnaissance, 1935* and Astill's *Mount Everest: The Reconnaissance 1935*	
1935	Kabru North	C. R. Cooke	Sirdar	Cooke's "The Ascent of Kabru"	The expedition made the first ascent of the mountain; Cooke was the only one to summit.
1936	Everest (North)	Hugh Ruttledge		Ruttledge's *Everest: The Unfinished Adventure*	
1936	Garhwal Himalaya	Eric Shipton	Sirdar	Shipton's "More Explorations Around Nanda Devi"	An attempt to climb Dunagiri while assisting Osmaston in survey of area
1937	First Karakoram (Shaksgam) Expedition	Eric Shipton	Sirdar	Shipton's *Blank on the Map* and Spender's "The Shaksgam Expedition, 1937"	Shaksgam and north side of K2. Ang Tharkay barely survived being swept down river while crossing.
1938	Everest (North)	Bill Tilman	Cook and Sirdar	Tilman's "Mount Everest 1938" and *Mount Everest 1938*	Ang Tharkay was awarded the Tiger Badge Award on May 30, 1939, as a result of his performance on this "light" expedition.
1939	Second Karakoram (Survey) Expedition	Eric Shipton	Sirdar	Russell's "The Karakoram Expedition, 1939," Shipton and Russell's "Karakorum, 1939," and Shipton's *Upon That Mountain*	The expedition, intended for sixteen months, was cut short due to the outbreak of WWII.
1945	Chomiomo (22,403 feet)	T. H. Tilly	Sirdar	Tilly and Noyce's "Chomiomo and Pauhunri"	Ang Tharkay summited.

Date	Destination	Expedition leader(s)	Role	Account	Notes
1945	Pauhunri (23,385 feet)	Wilfred Noyce	Sirdar	Noyce's *Mountains and Men* and Tilly and Noyce's "Chomiomo and Pauhunri"	Ang Tharkay summited.
1950	Annapurna	Maurice Herzog	Sirdar	Herzog's *Annapurna*	Ang Tharkay was awarded French Légion d'Honneur for his role in this climb.
1951	Everest (South)	Eric Shipton	Sirdar	Shipton's *The Mount Everest Reconnaissance Expedition, 1951*	
1952	Cho Oyu	Eric Shipton	Sirdar	Evans's "The Cho Oyu Expedition, 1952"	
1953	Dhaulagiri	Bernard Lauterburg	Sirdar	Roch's "Dhaulagiri, 1953" and Dyhrenfurth's *To the Third Pole*	Ang Tharkay broke through a cornice and fell roughly 100 meters on this Swiss expedition.
1953	Nun Kun	Bernard Pierre	Sirdar	Pierre's "Nun Kun" and *A Mountain Called Nun Kun*	Ang Tharkay broke ribs in an avalanche, so he was out of commission for final attempt.
1954	Rosenlaui, Switzerland	Naini D. Jayal, Principal of Himalayan Mountaineering Institute		Kapadia's "The Himalayan Mountaineering Institute Darjeeling"	Ang Tharkay became an instructor at the newly established Himalayan Mountaineering Institute in Darjeeling.
1954	Makalu	William Siri	Sirdar	Meyer and Lippmann's "First Attempt on Makalu, 1954"	
1955	Kamet	Naini D. Jayal	Sirdar	Jayal's "Early Years in Indian Mountaineering" and "Climbs and Expeditions: Asia, India, Kamet and Abi Gamin" (uncredited author)	The second successful ascent of Kamet
1962	Everest (South)	John Dias	Sirdar	Dias's *The Everest Adventure Story*	The expedition reached the South Col. This was Ang Tharkay's last active mountaineering.
1978	Dhaulagiri	Jean Coudray	Sirdar	Beghin's "Climbs and Expeditions: Asia, Nepal, Dhaulagiri, Southwest Buttress"	At the age of 70, Ang Tharkay participated in a final expedition. The team attempted the Southwest Buttress (also called the "South Buttress"), but reached only 7500 meters.

ENDNOTES

All notes are translated from the original edition (*Memoires d'un Sherpa*) unless otherwise noted. Brackets or "[—MB ed.]" indicate notes added for the Mountaineers Books edition.

Introduction to the Original Edition (1954)

1 It is unclear who Basil P. Norton was, or if there even was such a person. It may well be a pseudonym, which does nothing to resolve the mystery. Inquiries to the alpine clubs of both France and Great Britain, the Himalayan Club, and Maurice Herzog have come up blank. [—MB ed.]

2 "Sahib" is a Hindi word indicating a higher social status, used in everyday expedition language to distinguish between team members and Sherpas they have hired. Sherpas and coolies refer to the climbers as "sahibs," pronounced "saabs."

3 The 1954 American attempt on Makalu, led by Dr. William Siri, who would be part of the successful American ascent of Everest in 1963, reached an altitude of 23,500 feet before being forced to retreat. The team's report of the expedition in the *Himalayan Journal* includes this: "We were tremendously fortunate in having as sirdar, Ang Tharkey [*sic*], on whose shoulders also fell the responsibility of transport officer. A better man could not be found as this able Sherpa took over his duties with zeal." [—MB ed.]

PART I: CHILDHOOD AND FIRST EXPEDITIONS

Chapter 1: My Childhood

1 The year of Ang Tharkay's birth is listed in various sources as either 1907 or 1908. If he was born in the Year of the Monkey, then 1908 would be the correct year according to the Zodiac, which runs in twelve-year cycles. [—MB ed.]

2 Although the name "Ang" means "young," Ang Tharkay was the oldest child in his fam-
ily; "Young Tharkay" suggests an intergenerational distinction. Note also that within the
literature, the spelling of his name when translated is varied, including Ang Tharkey,
Angtharkay, Antarkay, Ang Tarke and Angtharkey. [—MB ed.]
3 A "dzong" is a kind of fortress found in Tibet and areas where Tibetan Buddhism is
common, such as Bhutan. They typically constitiute the religious, military, and adminis-
trative center for the surrounding district. [—MB ed.]
4 According to C. von Fürer Haimendorf, this inheritance practice, which Ang Tharkay
says is common in Khunde, is not the norm in all of Sherpa country. Often estates are
equally separated between sons.
5 The name of Ang Tharkay's youngest brother is spelled "Angphuter," "Angphuther," "Ang
Phuter," etc., in other books. (Pierre, *A Mountain Called Nun Kun*.)

CHAPTER 2: TRAVELS TO TIBET
1 The Nangpa La is a pass (at 5800 meters) that connects Tibet with the Sherpa region of
Nepal.

CHAPTER 3: SHERPA COUNTRY AND ITS INHABITANTS
1 Pumori is a distinct mountain, not an alternative name for Lobuche, which lies about
midway between Taboche (the modern name for Thobuche) and Pumori. Unlike the
comparatively tight-knit grouping of Everest, Lhotse, and Nuptse, the mountains in each
of these two groups are rather spread out. [—MB ed.]
2 "Tiger" is a title awarded by the Himalayan Club to Sherpas whose technique reaches a
sufficiently high level (Hunt, *The Ascent of Everest*). The use of the term began with the
1924 Everest expedition, where it was used for porters who went highest. [In 1939 the
Himalayan Club formalized the title, which was bestowed upon high-altitude porters,
based upon the recommendation of expedition leaders. Recipients were awarded a medal,
as well as a bonus of eight annas a day for work above the snowline. Ang Tharkay was
among the first group to formally receive the title and medal in 1939, based on his per-
formance on Everest with Tilman in 1938 (Hunt, *The Ascent of Everest*).]
3 While cumulatively, the successive German Nanga Parbat expeditions took a very high
toll in terms of lives, that of the 1934 expedition is significantly less than stated here: four
Germans and six Sherpa (Neale, *Tigers of the Snow*). [—MB ed.]
4 This Pemba Norbu is not the Sherpa by the same name who took part in the Everest
expeditions of 1951 and May 1952, Cho Oyu in 1952, and Nun Kun in August 1953.
5 Just as there are two Pemba Norbus, likewise there are two Pasang Phutars, the one men-
tioned here, who was born in 1929 and is one of Tenzing's cousins, and another Sherpa
born in 1910, a veteran of Kanchenjunga (1929), Everest (1933), Sikkim (Stoddart,
1935), Kabru (1935), Nanda Devi (1936), and Masherbrum (1938) expeditions.
6 This paragraph contains a few errors. First, Pasang Phutar lost his fingers due to frost-
bite incurred during his participation in the 1938 attempt on Masherbrun, led by J.O.M.

Roberts (Roberts, "The Attempt on Masherbrum, 1938"). Second, the other Sherpa referred to did not die "during that same expedition." Rather, this almost certainly refers to the Sherpa lost trying to bring Dudley Wolfe down from Camp VII during the 1939 American attempt on K2, Pasang Kitar (Kauffman and Putnam, *K2: The 1939 Tragedy*). Pasang Phutar was not on this expedition. Finally, three, not four, Sherpa died in this attempt: Pasang Kikuli, Phinsoo and Pasang Kitar. Pasang Kitar's remains were discovered on the mountain in 1993 (Payne, "Climbs and Expeditions: Asia, Pakistan, K2 Attempt, Rescue, Recovery of Bodies of Long-Lost Climbers and Micro-Hydroelectric Project."). [—MB ed.]

7 Here the reference is to the third attempt on the 1922 British expedition where, while attempting to gain the North Col, the climbers were hit by an avalanche. Of the nine Sherpas caught, seven (not six) were killed. Perhaps a sign of the times, none of them were named in the official account (Leigh-Mallory, "The Third Attempt"), and only one mentioned by name in the account by Howard Somervell, who wrote, "The first to be dug out was my servant, Narbu." (Somervell, *After Everest: The Experiences of a Mountaineer and Medical Missionary*, p. 72). [—MB ed.]

8 This is an error. There were six Sherpa on this expedition: Pasang Phuta, Nuri, Da Namgyal, Pasang Kikuli, and Nima Tsering. Only one, Kitar Dorje, died (in base camp) likely of dysentery or the result of food poisoning (Tilman, *The Ascent of Nanda Devi*; Neale, *Tigers of the Snow*). [—MB ed.]

9 We know four Sherpas named Ang Tsering. The one mentioned here, born in 1909, is Ang Tsering II, who died in the Nanga Parbat disaster in 1937. He had participated in Everest expeditions in 1933, 1935, and 1936, Kabru in 1935, and Nandakot [alternatively "Nanda Kot" or "Nanda Khat"] in 1936.

Two Sherpas named Kitar died in the mountains. A Kitar born in 1905 took part in many climbs, including Ruttledge's expedition to the Garhwal in 1932, and he was killed on Nanda Devi in 1936. Pasang Kitar died on K2 in 1939.

Pasang Kikuli was born in 1911 and died on K2 in 1939. He had taken part in expeditions to Kanchenjunga (1929, 1930, and 1931), Everest (1933), Nanga Parbat (1934), Nanda Devi (1936), and Sikkim (Cooke, "The Ascent of Kabru").

10 Ang Temba took part in the French expedition to the Karakoram in 1936. Another very famous Sherpa, born in 1932, has the same name and has participated in many expeditions since 1949. [Regarding the ages Ang Tharkay provides here, recall that he was narrating this in the early 1950s.]

11 Jigme Sherpa was killed by an avalanche on Nanga Parbat in 1937. He must not be confused with Jigme Tsering, who took part in the Kanchenjunga expeditions in 1929, 1930, and 1931, Nanga Parbat in 1934, the French expedition to the Karakoram in 1936, and [Klavs Becker-] Larsen's Everest expedition in 1951.

12 The 1937 German expedition to Nanga Parbat led by Karl Wien (Bauer, "Nanga Parbat, 1937") experienced the worst mountaineering accident up to that time. On June 14, while expedition members were sleeping, Camp IV was struck by a powerful avalanche that killed six German climbers (including Wien) and nine Sherpas who were at the camp. In this instance, the Sherpas were treated with respect and dignity: the "In Memoriam" article that appeared in *The Himalayan Journal* the following year

included brief biographical sketches and photographs for each: Pasang Norbu, Ang Tsering, Jigme (Jigmay) Sherpa, Nima Tsering, Gyaljen Monjo, Kami Sherpa, Chong Karma, Nim Tsering, and Mingma Tsering (Mason, "In Memoriam: The Porters Who Died on Nanga Parbat, 1937"). [—MB ed.]

13 This is an error in the original edition. The person referred to is T.H. Tilly. The mountain is question is more commonly known as Chomiomo, but also Chomoyummo. Ang Tharkay traveled there with Tilly in 1945. Tilly is quoted as saying that "he climbed Chomiomo mainly due to Angtharkay." [Aamir Ali. "*Himalayan Journal*: Vols XIII-XVII (1946-1954)"]. The following from Tilly's account speaks to Ang Tharkay's character and what he was like in the mountains, "Near the top Angtharkay unroped and positively rushed to the top at a speed which, at 22,400 feet, spoke volumes. Arrived, he rent the air with hideous screeches. Dawa Thondup and I followed, and the former added his contribution, in a small way, to the din." (Tilly & Noyce, "Chomiomo and Pauhunri"). [—MB ed.]

CHAPTER 4: I CHOOSE A CAREER AS A SHERPA

1 Born in 1900, this Gyalgen climbed in Sikkim with [Harold] Raeburn (1920), on Everest (1921, 1922, 1924), and on Kanchenjunga (1929, 1930). Seven other well-known Sherpas have the same name.

2 Ang Pasang, born in 1912, took part in the 1933 Everest expedition (Ruttledge, *Everest 1933*), the 1934 Sikkim expedition with [G. B.] Gourlay, (Anon., "Expeditions"), and the 1936 expedition to Tibet with [J. A. K.] Martyn. He died in 1943.

3 Born in 1900, Mingma Thu Thu, known as "Alice," accompanied expeditions to Everest in 1922 and 1924, to Kanchenjunga in 1931, to Sikkim (with [Gordon] Osmaston) in 1932 and to Rakaposhi in 1937 (with [Bill] Tilman). He disappeared on the return journey, probably as a result of the unrest in the country.

4 Eric Shipton notes in *Upon That Mountain* that his group traveled "via the 4,267-meter Natu-La." The two passes are about five kilometers apart, as the crow flies, and the two routes that Shipton and Ang Tharkay took meet up in Yatung. The ridges above these passes are listed on maps as having the following altitudes: Jelep-La, 4400 meters; near the Natu-La, 4728 meters.

CHAPTER 5: MY EXPEDITIONS TO EVEREST

1 This is apparently an error in the original edition. The correct number of Everest expeditions appears to be six: 1933, 1935, 1936, 1938, 1951, and 1962, so at the time the book was originally published, the number should have been five. [—MB ed.]

2 Shipton writes, "In Tsomgo." [Shipton, *Upon That Mountain*]

3 Camp IV had an altitude of approximately 7000 meters (ibid., 150).

4 On May 22, 1933, [Eugene St. John] Birnie, [John Edmund Hugh] Boustead, [Charles Raymond] Greene, and [Percy] Wyn Harris, with twenty porters carrying twenty kilos each, set up this camp (ibid., 151).

5 Rinsing Bhotia died in 1947; Pasang Bhotia died in 1948; Tsering Tharkay lived 1908–
 36. Camp VI, established on May 30, was at 8347 meters. In *Upon That Mountain*,
 Shipton praises the Sherpas: "He [Birnie] was helped a great deal in this by the remark-
 able courage and loyalty displayed by two of the old gang, Angtharkay and Kipa, who
 volunteered to go up again. It must be remembered that the Sherpas could not be
 expected to have the same feeling about the job that we had. These two had already done
 as much as could reasonably be expected of them. Their example was an inspiration to
 the other porters—and to us."

6 In *Upon That Mountain* Shipton, who had gone most of the way with him, writes that
 Smythe had reached 28,100 feet; Tony Smythe in *My Father, Frank*, quotes 28,200 feet as
 his father's high point. [—MB ed.]

7 Tenzing Norgay, also called Bhotia, was born in Thame, Nepal, in 1917 and is the world's
 most famous Sherpa. He is the most celebrated "tiger" and participated in many expedi-
 tions to Everest, the Garwhal, Sikkim, Chitral, Gangotri, the Karakoram, Nanda Devi,
 Nanga Parbat, and Bandar Punch. With Hillary, he conquered the summit of Everest on
 May 29, 1953. [Prior to joining the 1935 expedition, Tenzing had been a tenant in Ang
 Tharkay's house. Due to his lack of experience, he was not initially selected for the 1935
 expedition but was added when the number of Sherpas required increased.]

8 Tsering Tharkay started out on Kanchenjunga in 1929. He was on Everest in 1935
 and returned the next year. Tewang Bhotia died in 1942, having taken part in expedi-
 tions on Everest in 1924, 1933, 1934 ([Maurice] Wilson), 1935, and 1936, as well as on
 Kanchenjunga in 1929 and in Sikkim with [Paul] Bauer in 1936.

9 The North Col is at an altitude of 6800 meters. The climbers had planned to go up to
 8200 meters, but the bad weather and snow conditions did not allow this. (Shipton, *Upon
 That Mountain*).

10 Pasang Bhotia took part in the Everest expeditions in 1933, 1935, 1936, and 1938, and
 the 1934 Nanda Devi expedition. He died in 1948.

11 Norsang, known as "Policy," accompanied the Everest expeditions in 1922, 1924, 1933,
 and 1936, the 1932 Sikkim expedition (with Osmaston), the 1936 Nandakot [Nanda
 Kot] expedition, and the 1937 and 1938 Nanga Parbat expeditions. He died in 1942.

12 "Camp IV was established on the North Col early in May, but continuous bad weather
 compelled us to retreat," wrote Eric Shipton in *Upon That Mountain*.

13 This must be Kusang Sitar, who is described as follows in the Himalayan guide list: "Born
 in 1906. Expeditions: Kanchenjunga 1931; Everest 1933; Nanga Parbat 1934; Everest
 1935. Drowned crossing a river while returning from Everest." Ang Tharkay's memory
 might be incorrect, or perhaps there is an error in the notation. While the document lists
 1935 as the date of the last Everest expedition in which Kusang Sitar participated (and
 drowned on the return journey), Ang Tharkay states that this happened in 1936.

14 Tilman had a different view of Tharkay's abilities. In *Mount Everest 1938* he wrote, "Not
 that Angtharkay wanted very much instruction in the sort of cooking we should expect of
 him; his stews and curries had always been masterpieces, and, like most natives of India,
 he could, of course, turn out rice to perfection. . . . This year he added the duties of cook-
 ing for seven of us to his usual jobs of bossing up the porters, bestowing valuable advice
 and encouragement upon his employers, and carrying a heavier load farther and higher

than any one else if called upon to do so; in fact, a sort of Jeeves, Admirable Crichton, and Napoleon rolled into one, but taking himself less seriously than any of those redoubtable men." [—MB ed.]

15 Lobsang, awarded the Tiger Medal, had been on a climb in Shaksgam in 1937. He died on Zemu in 1945. There were two Sherpas named Gyalgen on Everest in 1938. One, called Mikchen, born in 1915, made multiple climbs. The other, born in 1918, would accompany Shipton to Mustagh Ata in 1947.

16 Born in 1913, Ang Karma participated in numerous expeditions: Everest in 1936 and 1938; Sikkim (with [Ernst] Grob) in 1939; "Lama Amden" in 1942; and Bandar Punch in 1943. He died during the war [World War II].

17 Camp IV was on the North Col, at the western foot of which lies the Rongbuk Glacier (Shipton, *Upon That Mountain*, p.185). After Tilman and Lloyd and fifteen Sherpas advanced to Camp VI, [Frank] Smythe and Shipton remained at Camp V with eight Sherpas.

18 Born in 1910, Nukku participated in Everest expeditions in 1936 and 1938, Shaksgam in 1937, and in Assam (with Tilman) in 1939. He died of malaria during the Assam expedition.

19 Of the five known Sherpas by this name, only Norbu Bhotia was on Everest in 1938. He had previously gone to Everest in 1936, and with Smythe to the Garhwal in 1937. He died in 1941.

20 This Pasang is Pasang Dawa Lama, also called Pasang Dawa Sherpa, born in 1911, recipient of the Tiger Medal, who took part in the following expeditions: Chomolhari in 1937; Sikkim in 1937 with Cooke; Masherbrum in 1938; K2 in 1939; Punjab in 1941 with [Jimmy] Roberts; Nanda Ghunti in 1944; Sasir in 1946 with Roberts; Pyramid in 1949; Chomo Yomo in 1950; Garhwal in 1950 with [Kenneth] Snelson; Mukut Parbat in 1951; Everest in 1951 with Shipton; and finally the Graaff expedition in 1952. On K2, he reached 8380 meters. Ang Tharkay did not specify which Nyima he refers to, and this name is very common among Sherpas.

21 Pumori is 7068 meters according to other surveys. [Currently accepted altitudes for these peaks, as given in Hawley and Salisbury (*The Himalayan Database: The Expedition Archives of Elizabeth Hawley*) are: Pumori (7165 m), Gyachung Kang (7952 m—the highest peak in the world that is not 8,000 m), Cho Oyu (8188 m), and Makalu (8485 m).]

22 Those heading to Pumori were [William H.] Murray, Riddiford, Bourdillon, and [Michael] Ward (Shipton, *The Mount Everest Reconnaissance Expedition, 1951*)

PART II, OTHER EXPEDITIONS

CHAPTER I: MY FIRST EXPEDITION TO NANDA DEVI

1 Eric Shipton provides a detailed account of this expedition in *Nanda Devi*.

2 This is not Kusang Sitar, who later drowned in the Arun River, but rather Kusang Namge, who was on Everest in 1933, on Nanda Devi in 1934 (the expedition described

here), and again on Everest in 1936 and 1938. He died around 1950 after being awarded the Tiger Medal.

3 On May 28 at nightfall (Shipton, *Upon That Mountain*).

4 The highest point of the Satopanth Glacier is at 7075 meters (according to Dyhrenfurth). Shipton writes (*Upon That Mountain*): "From the head of the Stopanth glacier we reached a saddle, 18,400 feet high, on the crest of the main watershed."

5 Probably the avalanche that Shipton describes in *Upon That Mountain*: "No sooner had we pitched the tents than there came a mighty roar from above and for fully a minute a cascade of huge ice blocks crashed down the gully sending up a spray of ice dust, while a number of ice splinters landed harmlessly on the tents." [—MB ed.]

CHAPTER 2: KUBRU

1 Ang Thari, Sherpa, was born in 1915. He took part in the Kabru expedition in 1935 and the Everest expedition in 1936.

CHAPTER 3: MY SECOND EXPEDITION TO NANDA DEVI

1 The account of this surveying expedition can be found in Eric Shipton's "More Explorations Round Nanda Devi." [—MB ed.]

2 The expedition included the Englishmen H. W. Tilman, T. Graham Brown, N. E. Odell, and Peter Lloyd, and the Americans Adams Carter, Arthur Emmons, W. F. Loomis, and Charles Houston (Shipton, *Upon That Mountain*).

3 With the exception of Tilman and Houston, who left Nanda Devi separately from the other group in order to explore a new route out of the sanctuary. Tilman writes in chapter 17 of *The Ascent of Nanda Devi*, "I was bent on attempting to force a new route out of the Basin by 'Longstaff's Col' and Houston was keen to come too." [—MB ed.]

4 Dunagiri is 7065 meters.

5 The woman was Pamela Freston. Her romantic relationship with Shipton spanned 1936–1939; they not only maintained a correspondence for the rest of his life, she also edited the manuscripts of his books, starting with *Blank on the Map*. [—MB ed.]

CHAPTER 4: MY FIRST JOURNEY TO THE KARAKORAM

1 The Hindu Kush, Karakoram, and Himalaya are considered three separate ranges. [—MB ed.]

2 More commonly referred to as "Raksi or "Rakshi," this is a rather strong fermented spirit, not a wine. It is made from rice or millet. [—MB ed.]

3 There is, in fact, no village after Askole, much less one from which you can see the Baltoro. There is, however, Paiju camp, which is very close to the end of the Baltoro glacier moraine. This is almost certainly what is being referred to. [—MB ed.]

4 K2 is the world's second-highest summit (8611 meters according to some surveys, 8591 according to others). It was conquered by the Italians in 1954. It has been called by many

names, including Mount Godwin Austen and Chogori (in Balti: Great Mountain) (G. O. Dyhrenfurth, *To the Third Pole*).

5 Lhakpa Tenzing, born in 1915, took part in expeditions to Everest (1933), Kabru (1935), Karakoram (French expedition in 1936), Shaksgam (1937), and Everest again (1938). He was awarded the Tiger Medal.

6 Many Sherpas have or had this name. This Lobsang was born in 1909. He was on the 1938 expedition to Everest, was awarded the Tiger Medal, and died in Zemu in 1945.

CHAPTER 5: MY SECOND EXPEDITION TO THE KARAKORAM

1 In addition to Eric Shipton, the team included Scott Russell (climber / botanist), Eadric Fountained (doctor), and Peter Mott (surveyor), as well as two Indian surveyors, Fazall Ellahi and Inayat Khan. (See Shipton and Russell's "Karakorum, 1939" and also Shipton's *Upon That Mountain.*) [—MB ed.]

PART III: ANNAPURNA

CHAPTER 1: MY FIRST CONTACT WITH THE FRENCH EXPEDITION

1 Francis Deloche de Noyelle. [A French diplomat who had been a member of the French Resistance during World War II. A member of the 1950 French Annapurna Expedition, he served in the role of liaison officer.]

2 We know of five Sherpas named Ang Dawa. The one referred to here is Ang Dawa number four, referred to as Chota, who had been on an expedition to Pyramid in 1949 and who took part in [René] Dittert's expedition to the Garhwal in 1950, Nanda Devi and Yalung in 1951, and Everest in 1952.

3 Ang Tsering ("Pansy"), born in 1907, also explored Everest in 1936, the Garhwal in 1937, Sikkim in 1937 and 1939, Pyramid in 1949, Nanda Devi in 1951, and Kamet in 1952. He was awarded the Tiger Medal.

Dawa Thondup, born in 1907, also took part in expeditions to Everest in 1933, 1936, and 1952 (up to 8000 meters); Garhwal in 1935 (Auden); Sikkim in 1937 (Cooke); Masherbrum in 1938; K2 in 1939; "Lama Amden" in 1942; Bandar Punch in 1943, 1944, and 1946; Chomo Yomo in 1945; Nilkanta in 1947 (Wylie); Gangotri in 1947 (Roch); Pyramid and Kanchengyao in 1946; Abi Gamin in that same year (Dittert); and Trisul in 1951. He was awarded the Tiger Medal. His name is also written Dawa Thundu, Dawa Thendup, Dawatoundu, etc.

Sarki, born in 1920, also took part in the expeditions to Nun-Kun and Chomo Yomo in 1946, the Khumbu in 1950 with Houston, Nanda Devi in 1951, and Everest in 1952 (up to 8000 meters).

Fou Tharkay, born in 1922, took part in expeditions to Panhunri (1945); Rakaposhi (1947); Nepal (with Tilman) in 1949; Karakoram and Nanga Parbat (with [R. M. W.]

Marsh), 1950–51; Trisul (1951); Talung (with Frey) in 1951; and Everest (up to 8000 meters) in 1952. His name is sometimes written Phou (or Phu) Tharkay (or Tharke).

Aïla, born in 1911, also took part on expeditions to Everest, 1936, 1951 (with [Becker-] Larsen), and 1952 (up to 7500 meters); Shaksgam (1937); Gangotri (Austrian expedition) in 1938; Sikkim (with Grob) in 1939; Pyramid (1949); and Kulu (1951). He was awarded the Tiger Medal. Further on, Ang Tharkay says that Aïla is brother of Ang Tsering (Pansy).

Adjiba (or Ajiba), born in 1911, also took part in expeditions to Everest in 1933, 1936, 1951 (Becker-Larsen), and 1952 (up to 8000 meters); Kabru (1935); Rakaposhi (1938; Sikkim (with Grob) in 1937 and 1939; Pyramid and Kangchengayao (1949), Karakoram and Nanga Parbat (Marsh) in 1950–51; and Kulu (1951).

CHAPTER 2: EN ROUTE
1 "Pansy" was the nickname for Ang Tsering, used to distinguish him from three other Sherpas by the same name.
2 There are at least two villages named Tukucha (also spelled "Tukuche") in Nepal. The village referred to here is very small and lies on the Annapurna Circuit trekking trail, about midway between Annapurna to Dhaulagiri, north of the village of Lete. [—MB ed.]
3 April 24, 1950 (Herzog, *Annapurna*).

CHAPTER 3: RECONNAISSANCE
1 Mount Tukucha is at an altitude of 6915 [6920] meters. The village of Tukucha is at approximately 2580 meters.
2 April 26 (Herzog, *Annapurna*).
3 In *Annapurna*, Herzog sets May 17 as the date of Ang Tharkay's arrival in Muktinath.
4 In Muktinath, there were "two narrow apertures. Along them came the sound of the flowing water, and in them flickered the blue flame of a natural gas which burned perpetually" (Herzog, *Annapurna*).
5 At 5100 meters, according to Herzog's *Annapurna*.

CHAPTER 4: THE ASSAULT
1 At 6600 meters (Herzog, *Annapurna*).
2 At 5900 meters (ibid.).
3 At 7150 meters (ibid.).

CHAPTER 5: VICTORY
1 June 3, 1950. [Note also that the altitude is higher than stated: 8091 meters.]
2 (Herzog, *Annapurna*).

CHAPTER 6: THE RETURN

1 Krishna Gandaki is another name for the previously mentioned Kali Gandaki.

EPILOGUE: NUN KUN

1 Claude Kogan was the female member of the expedition, the memsahib (madam sahib). [The six Sherpa were Gyaldzen, Pemba Norbu, Kami, Ang Phuter, Pa Norbo, and Ang Tharkay. The "four sahibs" were Bernard Pierre (leader, or "bara sahib"), Michel Desorbay, Dr. Jean Guillemin, and Pierre Vittoz ("pastor sahib"). The two Indian officers were Captain K.C. Johorey and Lietenant N.D. Jayal, who the next year would become principal of Himalayan Mountaineering Institute in Darjeeling, where Ang Tharkay would be an instructor, and with whom Ang Tharkay would travel to Rosenlaui, Switzerland, to take courses at the Swiss Mountaineering School.]

2 (Pierre, *A Mountain Called Nun Kun*)

3 August 10, 1953.

4 Ang Tharkay suffered broken ribs and contusions in the avalanche, and despite these injuries, assisted Michel Desorbay—a rather strong indication of his character. (ibid., pp. 150-154). [—MB ed.]

5 Kami, who was then twenty-one years old, was the youngest expedition member (ibid., p. 25). In the annals of Himalayan climbing are references to another Sherpa by the same name, who died in 1931 on the return from Kanchenjunga.

6 "Helen Memsahib" refers to an Englishwoman who lived in Srinagar, who supported expeditions in the Karakoram, mainly Shipton's.

BIBLIOGRAPHY

Ali, Aamir. *"Himalayan Journal*: Vols XIII-XVII (1946-1954)." *The Himalayan Journal*, Vol. 52, edited by Harish Kapadia (1996): 145-180. https://www.himalayanclub.org/hj/52/19/himalayan-journal-vols-xiii -xviii-1946-1954/

Anonymous. "Expeditions." *The Himalayan Journal*, Vol. 7, edited by Kenneth Mason (1935) https://www.himalayanclub.org/hj/07/14/expeditions-7/

> A summary of the expedition in northeastern Sikkim undertaken by G. B. Gourlay and J. B. Auden in October and early November 1934.

Anonymous. "Climbs and Expeditions: Asia, India, Kamet and Abi Gamin." *The American Alpine Journal*, Vol. 10, no. 1 (1956): 142. http://aac -publications.s3.amazonaws.com/documents/aaj/1956/PDF /AAJ_1956_10_1_142a.pdf

Astill, Tony. *Mount Everest: The Reconnaissance 1935: The Forgotten Adventure*. Privately published, 2005.

Bauer, Paul. "Nanga Parbat, 1937." *The Himalayan Journal*, Vol. 10, edited by Kenneth Mason, (1938) https://www.himalayanclub.org/hj/10/9 /nanga-parbat-1937/

———. *Kanchenjunga Challenge*. London: William Kimber, 1955.

Becker-Larsen, Klavs. *Everest Udfordringen.* Bagsværd, Denmark: Forlaget Amanda, 1991.

> An account (in Danish) of Becker-Larsen's 1951 unsanctioned solo attempt on Everest, based on his diaries.

Beghin, Pierre. "Climbs and Expeditions: Asia, Nepal, Dhaulagiri, Southwest Buttress." *American Alpine Journal,* Vol. 23, no. 55: 271–272, (1981) http://aac-publications.s3.amazonaws.com/documents/aaj/1981/PDF /AAJ_1981_23_55_271.pdf

Cooke, C.R. "The Ascent of Kabru." *The Himalayan Journal,* Vol. 8, edited by Kenneth Mason, (1936): 107–117 https://www.himalayanclub.org /hj/08/12/the-ascent-of-kabru/

> This article is worth looking up, even if only for the photos, which give an excellent sense of what they faced in terms of the ice fall and seracs. As Cooke was the only member of the expedition to summit, this has at times been referred to as the highest solo climb until 1953; however, since there was support up to the high camp (VI), and Cooke was accompanied by Schabarth partway on the final push above, on summit day, this would count as a "solo ascent" only in the most generous sense of the term (which takes nothing away from the accomplishment).

Dias, John. *The Everest Adventure: Story of the Second Indian Expedition.* Delhi: Publications Division, Ministry of Information and Broadcasting, 1965.

Dyhrenfurth, G.O. *To the Third Pole.* London: Werner Laurie, 1955. www.archive.org/stream/tothethirdpole029954mbp/tothethirdpole 029954mbp_djvu.txt

> A history of early attempts on the mountains above 26,000 feet, which Dyhrenfurth considers to be—in terms of a goal—the "third pole."

Evans, R.C. "The Cho Oyo Expedition, 1952." *The Alpine Journal,* Vol. 59 (1953): 9–18. www.alpinejournal.org.uk/Contents/Contents_1953_files /AJ59%201953%209-18%20Evans%20Cho%20Oyu.pdf

> What is interesting is that Ang Tharkay is not mentioned in this article.

Fisher, James F.. *Sherpas: Reflections on Change in Himalayan Nepal.* Berkeley: University of California, 1990.

An anthropological study of the Sherpa.

Fürer-Haimendorf, C. von. *The Sherpas of Nepal: Buddhist Highlanders.* Calcutta: Oxford Book Co, 1964.

This is the first anthropological study of the Sherpa.

Hawley, Elizabeth and Richard Salisbury. *The Himalayan Database: The Expedition Archives of Elizabeth Hawley.* Golden, CO: American Alpine Club, 2004.

This is a comprehensive searchable database on CD-ROM that has been built from Hawley's archives. It also includes a table detailing the literature that relates to the expeditions and data on peaks such as elevation.

Herzog, Maurice. *Annapurna Premier 8000.* Grenoble: Arthaud, 1951.

———. *Annapurna.* Guilford, CT: Lyons Press, 1997. First published 1952 by Jonathan Cape.

The previous two entries are the French and English language editions of Herzog's classic—the former used to check and compare quotes, etc. in this volume.

Herzog, Maurice and Marcel Ichac. *Regards vers l'Annapurna.* Grenoble: Arthaud, 1951.

A collection of photographs documenting the 1951 French expedition to Annapurna, this is a valuable supplement to Herzog's expedition book. While the brief introductory text, and annotations of the photos are in French, the basic captions are straightforward, and the photos speak for themselves.

Hunt, John. *The Ascent of Everest.* London: Hodder & Stoughton, 1953.

Ives, Katie. "Between the Lines." *Alpinist,* Vol. 51, (Autumn 2015): 11–12. http://dev.alpinist.com/doc/web15x/sharp-end-katie-ives

Jayal, Naini D. "Early Years of Indian Mountaineering." *The Himalayan Journal,* Vol. 62, edited by Harish Kapadia, (2006). https://www.himalayanclub.org/hj/62/16/early-years-of-indian-mountaineering/

Kapadia, Harish. "The Himalayan Mountaineering Institute Darjeeling." *The Alpine Journal,* Vol. 99, edited by Johanna Merz (1994): 225–227.

Kauffman, Andrew and William Putnam. *K2: The 1939 Tragedy.* Seattle: Mountaineers Books, 1992.

Keay, John. *The Great Arc: The Dramatic Tale of How India Was Mapped and Everest Was Named.* New York: Harper Collins, 2000.

Kohli , M.S. *Sherpas: The Himalayan Legends.* New Delhi: UBS Publishers, 2003.

Leigh-Mallory, G. A. "The Third Attempt" in *The Assault on Mount Everest, 1922,* edited by Charles Granville Bruce. (London: Longmans, Green & Co., 1923) 273–286.

Lhatoo, Dorjee. "Climbing Sherpas of Darjeeling." *The Himalayan Journal,* Vol. 35, edited by Soli S. Mehta (1979). https://www.himalayanclub .org/hj/35/34/climbing-sherpas-of-darjeeling/

———. "In Memoriam: Ang Tharkay." *The Himalayan Journal,* Vol. 39, edited by Harish Kapadia (1983). https://www.himalayanclub.org /hj/39/25/in-memoriam-39/

Mason, Kenneth. "In Memoriam: The Porters Who Died on Nanga Parbat, 1937." *The Himalayan Journal, Vol. 10. edited by Kenneth Mason (1938) https://www.himalayanclub.org/hj/10/14/in-memoriam-23/*

Messner, Reinhold. *Annapurna: 50 Years of Expeditions in the Death Zone.* Seattle: Mountaineers Books, 2000.

> This is a short, uneven book that is mainly written in support of Herzog (1952), in response to criticisms, such as those of David Roberts in *True Summit* (although Roberts is never mentioned). The book also documents a number of other key ascents of Annapurna, including that of Messner and Hans Kammerlander of the northwest face in 1985. Although the book is written in support of Herzog, he does not come off very well. Nevertheless, it is a good counterpoint to the Herzog and Roberts volumes.

Meyer, L. Bruce and Fritz Lippmann. "First Attempt on Makalu, 1954." *The Himalayan Journal,* Vol. 19, edited by H.W. Tobin, (1956). www .himalayanclub.org/hj/19/4/first-attempt-on-makalu-1954/

Neale, Jonathan. *Tigers of the Snow: How One Fateful Climb Made the Sherpas Mountaineering Legends.* London: Little Brown, 2002.

> This book attempts to tell the story of mountaineering from the Sherpas' perspective. The centerpiece is an account of the German attempt on Nanga Parbat in 1934, which the author argues was a turning point in how the Sherpas perceived themselves, relative to the European mountaineers who employed them. The book includes considerable detail on Sherpa life and customs.

Norgay, Tenzing and James Ullman. *Tiger of the Snow.* New York: G.P. Putnam's Sons, 1955.

> This is an autobiography of Tenzing Norgay Sherpa who, with Sir Edmund Hillary, made the first successful ascent of Mount Everest. Although Tenzing could neither read nor write, he was clearly an exceptional man, not only for his climbing, but for his character and intelligence as well. While his story was put down on paper by Ullman, Tenzing's voice and thoughts come through convincingly.

> Tenzing spends very little time on the actual climb in 1953, simply saying that others have written extensively about it, so there is no need to cover the details of the expedition, other than to shed light on things that have been neglected. Instead, unlike other expedition members at the time, he discusses the issues of conflict between the Sherpas and "sahibs," as well as the repercussions (since many of these caused controversy under the scrutiny that fell on the expedition after its success.) He also covers, in some depth, the significant impact of the expedition and its aftermath on his life.

Noyce, Wilfred. *Mountains and Men.* London: Geoffrey Bles, 1947.

> Contains a brief chapter on Ang Tharkay and the 1945 reconnaissance of Pauhunri. While respectful, his characterization is not overly flattering.

———. *South Col: One Man's Adventure on the Ascent of Everest, 1953.* London: William Heinemann, 1954.

> Has a brief section (pp. 32–33) in which the author contrasts the character of Tenzing Norgay and Ang Tharkay.

Ortner, Sherry B. *Sherpas Through Their Rituals.* Cambridge: Cambridge University Press, 1978.

———. *High Religion: A Cultural and Political History of Sherpa Buddhism.* Princeton, NJ: Princeton University Press, 1989.

Describes the building of Tengboche Monastery in 1916, the first of five major Sherpa monasteries in the Solu-Khumbu region of Nepal.

———. *Life and Death on Mt. Everest: Sherpas and Himalayan Mountaineering.* Princeton, NJ: Princeton University Press, 1999.

Despite the title, it is not really a book on climbing, mountaineering or Mount Everest; rather, it is anthropological study of the Sherpa people. Specifically, Ortner examines the influence that climbers and mountaineering have had on Sherpa life and culture since the first expedition in 1921. This is an excellent source for those interested in Sherpa culture, and it sheds good insights into the changes in the culture of the climbers themselves.

Payne, Roger. "Climbs and Expeditions: Asia, Pakistan, K2 Attempt, Rescue, Recovery of Bodies of Long-Lost Climbers and Micro-Hydroelectric Project." *American Alpine Journal,* Vol. 36, no. 68 (1994): 247. http://publications.americanalpineclub.org/articles/12199424701

Pierre, Bernard. *A Mountain Called Nun Kun.* London: Hodder & Stoughton, 1955.

———. "Nun-Kun." *American Alpine Journal,* Vol. 9, no. 1 (1954): 29. http://publications.americanalpineclub.org/articles/12195402900/Nun-Kun

Richardus, Peter (Ed.) *Tibetan Lives: Three Himalayan Autobiographies.* Richmond, UK: Curzon Press, 1998.

A compilation of the autobiographies of three individuals—Phu-tshogs Lung-rtogs, Karma Sum-dhon Paul, and Ts'an-chih Chen—who served as intermediaries for the British in their dealings with Tibet around the beginning of the twentieth century. Karma Paul is the best known of the three in mountaineering circles; he worked with many British expeditions and Sherpas, including Ang Tharkay.

Roberts, David. *True Summit: What Really Happened on the Legendary Ascent of Annapurna*. New York: Simon & Schuster, 2000.

> This book presents a revisionist account of the first ascent of Anna-purna as described in Herzog's book. It makes a very strong case that things were not as ideal or heroic as they had been painted. A key assertion is that the contribution of the other team members, especially Louis Lachenal, were systematically downplayed in order to better advance the narrative of a team following their leader in the united pursuit of a great objective.

Roberts, J.O.M. "The Attempt on Masherbrum, 1938." *The Hima-layan Journal,* Vol. 11, edited by Kenneth Mason, (1939). www .himalayanclub.org/hj/11/3/the-attempt-on-masherbrum-1938/

Roch, André. "Dhaulagiri, 1953." *The Himalayan Journal,*Vol. 18, edited by H.W. Tobin, (1954). www.himalayanclub.org/hj/18/8/dhaulagiri-1953/

Russell, R. Scott. "The Karakoram Expedition, 1939." *Alpine Journal* 52 (1940): 195–208. http://alpinejournal.org.uk/Contents/Contents_1940 _files/AJ52%201940%20195-208%20Scott%20Russell%20 Karakoram%201939.pdf

> A very good description of the expedition, illustrated with excellent photographs.

Ruttledge, Hugh. *Everest 1933*. London: Hodder & Stoughton, 1934.

———. *Everest: The Unfinished Adventure*. London: Hodder & Stoughton, 1937.

Shipton, Eric. *Blank on the Map*. London: Hodder & Stoughton, 1938.

———. "More Explorations Round Nanda Devi." *The Geographical Journal,* Vol. 90, no. 2 (1937): 97–107.

———. "The Mount Everest Reconnaissance, 1935." *The Himalayan Jour-nal,* Vol. 8, edited by Kenneth Mason, (1936). https://www.himalayan club.org/hj/11/1/mount-everest/

———. *The Mount Everest Reconnaissance Expedition, 1951*. London: Hodder & Stoughton, 1952.

———. *Nanda Devi.* London: Hodder & Stoughton, 1936.

———. *The Six Mountain-Travel Books.* Seattle: Mountaineers Books, 1985.

———. *That Untravelled World: An Autobiography.* Seattle: Mountaineers Books, 2015. First published 1969 by Hodder & Stoughton.

———. *Upon That Mountain.* London: Hodder & Stoughton, 1943.

Shipton, Eric and Scott R. Russell. "Karakorum, 1939." *Geographical Journal,* Vol. 95, no.1 (1940): 409–427.

Shipton, Eric and H.W. Tilman. *Nanda Devi: Exploration and Ascent.* Seattle: Mountaineers Books, 2000.

> A single volume containing Shipton's *Nanda Devi* and Tilman's *The Ascent of Nanda Devi.*

Smythe, Tony. *My Father, Frank.* Seattle: Mountaineers Books, 2015. First published 2013 by Bâton Wicks.

Somervell, T. Howard. *After Everest: The Experiences of a Mountaineer and Medical Missionary.* London: Hodder & Stoughton, 1936.

Spender, M. "The Shaksgam Expedition, 1937." *The Himalayan Journal,* Vol. 10. edited by Kenneth Mason, (1938). https://www.himalayanclub .org/hj/10/2/the-shaksgam-expedition-1937/

Steele, Peter. *Eric Shipton: Everest and Beyond.* Seattle: Mountaineers Books, 1998.

> A very well-researched biography of Eric Shipton that draws on his correspondence and expedition reports.

Terray, Lionel. *Conquistadors of the Useless.* Seattle: Mountaineers Books, 2001. First published 1963 by Victor Gollancz.

> One of the best books in all of mountaineering literature, this is the autobiography of Lionel Terray, a key member of the 1950 French Annapurna expedition. Snowblind high on the mountain, Terray was led down to Camp IV and safety by Ang Tharkay.

Tilly, T. H. and G.W.F. Noyce. "Chomiomo and Pauhunri." *The Himalayan Journal,* Vol. 13, edited by G.W.F. Noyce, (1946). https://www.himalayan club.org/hj/13/6/chomiomo-and-pauhunri/

Tilman, H.W. *The Ascent of Nanda Devi.* New York: The Macmillan Company, 1937.

————. "Mount Everest, 1938." *The Himalayan Journal,* Vol. 11, edited by Kenneth Mason, (1939). www.himalayanclub.org/hj/11/1/mount -everest/

————. *Mount Everest 1938.* Cambridge: Cambridge University Press, 1948.

————. *The Seven Mountain-Travel Books.* Seattle: Mountaineers Books, 1983.

————. *When Men and Mountains Meet.* Cambridge: Cambridge University Press, 1946.

Ward, Michael. "The Great Angtharkay." *The Alpine Journal,* Vol. 101 (1996): 182–186. http://alpinejournal.org.uk/Contents/Contents_1996 _files/AJ 1996 182-186 Ward Angtharkay.pdf

INDEX

"n" indicates the reference appears in a note

Adjiiba, 120–21, 126, 131,
 135–36, 145–46, 149, 189n3
Aïla, 120–21, 124, 126, 135,
 138, 140, 189n3
alcohol, 24
Algarah, 28
Alps, 154
Ama Dablam, 37
Annapurna, 13, 114, 117–59
Annapurna, 14, 189n3
Arun River, 47, 66
Arun valley, 63
Askole, 101–03
Auden, John, 104–05
Austen, Godwin, 42
avalanches, 7, 42, 77, 105, 163,
 168, 187n5

Badrinath, 85
Baglung, 124, 128
Baijnath, 84
Baltoro, 102
Baltoro Glacier, 102
bamboo, 86
Banduk, 148
Bangdel, L. S., 155–59
Bauer, Paul, 179
Beirut, 154
Benares, 48
Beni, 124, 133, 148
Bhotey Butsy, 151
Bhotia, Kusang, 66, 83, 88
Bhotia, Pasang, 57, 64, 71–72,
 77, 83, 86, 88, 185n8
Bhotia, Rinsing, 57, 185n5
Bhotia, Tewang, 62
Bhutan, 51
Biratnagar, 74
Birne, E. St. J., 57

birth of children, 39
Bombay, 97
Bonu, 42
Bourdillon, Tom, 77–78
Braham, Trevor, 173
Bruce, C. G., 40
Buddha, 131–32
Buddhism, 36
Buddhist monasteries, 31
Butwal, 121, 150

Calcutta, 83, 98, 153–54
Cha-ba, 36
Chadziou Khola, 147
Chamoli, 87
Chang-Thang, 63
Chatuck, 75
chauri cows, 26
Chering, Ang, 42–43
Chhu La Mebar, 132
Chhule, 30
Chhu-Sherpa, 36
childhood, 21–28
Chi-Long-Mamo, 55
Ching-Thung, 49
Chipko, 30
Cho Dzong, 70
Cho Oyu, 37, 78
Chomo Yomo, 43
Chowk Bazaar, 48
Choya, 147
Chubrang, 91
chuk-tuk, 26
Chumbah La, 91
Chuttok La, 35
Cooke, C. R., 91, 93, 170, 179
coolies, 74–76, 84, 88, 100–01,
 103, 121, 123–24, 135, 145–
 46, 148–49, 162, 164–65

Couzy, Jean, 120, 140, 142, 144
cows, 26
Cranston, R. S., 170
cremation, 39
crevasses, 7, 41
crime, 39

Daiju, 102
Daman, 175
Dambush Khola, 125–26
Dana, 124, 148
Darjeeling, 8, 27–28, 34, 42,
 45–49, 51, 58–60, 63–64,
 72–73, 78, 89, 91–93, 98–99,
 109, 112, 117, 132, 151, 153,
 158, 165, 175–76
Darjeeling Himalayan Club,
 153
Da-Te, 22
Dawa, Ang, 95, 118, 120–21,
 131, 188n2
Delhi, 150
Desorbay, Michel, 163
Devies, Lucien, 157, 159
Dhabar, 131
Dhankuta, 74
dharamsala, 30–31, 87, 132
Dharan, 74
Dhaulagiri, 124, 126–27, 129
Diksha, 60
Dingla, 74–75
Dje Naza, 31
Do La Mebar, 132
dochas, 24
Doda, 161
Dong Kung, 68
Dorje, Ang, 78
Dorje, Nim, 42, 57
dowry, 38

Dudh Kosi, 34, 40
Dum Dum, 154
Dunagiri, 96
Dutta, Mr., 78
dysentery, 26–27
Dzong, Phari, 28
Dzong-Ri, 91

East Rongbuk glacier, 41
Eiffel Tower, 158
Elephanta, 97
Everest, 9–10, 13, 34, 37, 40
 fifth expedition to (1951),
 73–78
 first expedition to (1933), 51,
 53–59
 fourth expedition to (1938),
 67–73
 second expedition to (1935),
 59–63
 third expedition to (1936),
 64–67
Everest 1933, 14, 40, 59
Everest 1938, 14

father, 21–22, 24, 26
Faucille Glacier, 136
festivals, 37–38
Folies-Bergère, 158
Fontainebleau forest, 157
food, 23, 36–37
French Alpine Club, 156, 158
French Mountain Federation,
 157, 159
Freston, Pamela, 187n5
frostbite, 7, 12, 58, 141

Gandaki River, 131
Ganges, 85
Gangtok, 49, 59–60, 63
Garhwal, 74
Garomboree, 148
Gatch, 104
Gatung Paga, 63
Gautsa, 53
Ghar-ja, 36
Gharti, 36
Ghasa, 125
Gilgit, 43, 106–07, 109, 112
Giru, 68
Go-farma, 36
Goi Khaska Khola, 75
Goley, 36
Gompa Lhabu, 60, 68–69
grasses, 37

Great Frozen Lake, 129
Green Lake, 49
Gurkha, 149
Gwaldam, 84
Gyachung Kang, 78
Gyalgen, 46, 48, 68, 111
Gyantsé, 61

Hanzale, 162
Harris, Wyn, 57
Herzog, Maurice, 13–14, 119,
 123, 125–30, 136, 142, 144,
 153, 156, 158
Hillary, Edmund, 13, 53, 77–78
Himalayan Club, 48, 50, 60,
 98, 154
Himalayan Institute of Moun-
 taineering, 175
Himalayas, 8–9, 11, 13–14, 27,
 51, 99, 102, 107, 117, 122,
 126, 154–55
Hindukush, 99
Hindustani, 106
Hishe, 42
Hispar Glacier, 112
Hunt, John, 42
Hunza valley, 107, 109

Ichac, Marcel, 120, 126–27,
 129–30, 133, 135–36, 141,
 155–57
Ihawa, 36
Ilam, 47
illness, 49
Imja Khola valley, 35
Indian Topographic Service, 78,
 95, 109, 162
Indus valley, 100

Ja Po Wa, 31
Ja Tsampa, 31
Jamaraja, 132
Jammu, 161
jaundice, 49–50
Jayanagar, 23–24
Jelep-La, 51
Jigme, 43, 46–47, 183n11
Jogbani, 73–74
Joshimath, 84–85, 96

K2, 102, 107, 187n4
Kabru, 91–93
Kali Gandaki, 123–24
Kalimpong, 28, 50, 64, 67, 98,
 132

Kalung, 75
Kamba, 36
Kamri col, 109
Kanchenjunga, 11, 49, 62
Kangtepa, 37
Kapup, 28
Karachi, 154
Karakoram, 8, 14, 40, 170
 first expedition to, 99–107
 map of, 108
 second expedition to, 109–12
Kargil, 100
Karma, Ang, 70, 186n16
Kashmir, 43, 100, 107, 161
Kathgodam, 83, 95
Kathmandu, 14, 34, 78,
 150–51, 175
Kedarnath, 85, 87
Kempe, Geo E., 170
Khamba, 35
Khamba Dzong, 54, 68
Khamba-chen, 36
Khari-Khola, 46
Kharta valley, 62–63, 66, 72
khata, 38, 61, 70
Khumbu, 8, 21, 26, 35, 39,
 59, 76
Khumbu Glacier, 76–77
Khumjung, 34
Khunde, 21, 25–27, 29, 34, 45
Kikuli, Pasang, 42
Kirat tribe, 35, 47
Kishtwar, 161–62
Kitar, 42
Kogan, Claude, 165, 190n1
Kohli, M.S., 7, 175
Koktang Glacier, 91
Kori La, 35
Kosisagar, 24
Krishna Gandaki, 147–48
Kungo Raba, 30
Kusma, 148
Kyetrak, 29, 31
Kyishong, 64

Lachen, 60, 68, 70
Lachenal, Louis, 120, 129, 131,
 133, 136, 140, 142, 144–46,
 148
Ladakh, 161
lama(s), 37–39, 58, 65, 76, 128,
 131
Lama, Kipa, 56–57
Lama, Pasang Dawa, 186n20
Lamaism, 36

Lama-murmin, 36
language, 11, 35
Leba, 58
Lete, 125, 147
Lhotse, 37, 77
livestock, 35–36, 40
Lobsang, 103–04, 111, 176, 186n15
Lobuche, 37, 76, 78
Lobuche-Khola valley, 77
Longland, John Laurence, 57
Lopara, 162
Losar, 38
Lucknow, 83, 118–19
Lunak, 30–31, 63

Maharajah, 150
Maiktoli, 88
Makalu, 78
Mallory, George, 40, 42
Manangbhot, 128–30
Marignan cinema, 156
marriage, 28, 38–39
Mayangdi Khola, 124
Mélong, 132
memsahib, 162–64
Memsahib, Helen, 165
Men-de, 36
Metro, 158
Miristi Khola, 120, 124
Morris, John, 64, 73
mother, 21–23, 27
Mount Everest. *See* Everest
Mount Everest Reconnaissance Expedition, 1951, 14, 33, 73
Mount Makalu, 34
Mount Tukucha, 127, 189n1
mountaineering, 8
Muk, 60
Mukerjee, Mohan Lal, 11–12
Muktinath, 128–32, 136
Muktinath Himal, 130
mules, 34
Mundal, 87
Murray, Mr., 78

Nagar, 109
Nagir, 112
Namche Bazaar, 14, 26–27, 34–35, 39–40, 46, 73, 76
Namge, Kusang, 186n2
Namgyal, Agu Da, 10
Nanda Devi, 14, 42, 60, 80, 169
 first expedition to, 83–89
 second expedition to, 95–98

Nanga Parbat, 42–43, 46, 83, 89, 109, 182n3, 183n12
Nangpa La, 29, 31, 34, 37, 78
Napachi, 162, 165
Nautanwa, 118, 120–21, 150
Nepal, 8, 14, 16–17, 34, 73, 83, 124, 149
New Delhi, 161
Norbu, Pemba, 42, 164, 182n4
Norbu, Wangdi, 54, 66
Norgay, Tenzing, 7, 9, 13, 53, 60–61, 78, 185n7
Norsang, 64, 185n11
North Col, 8, 40, 62–63, 183n7, 185n9, 186n17
Norton, Edward, 40
Noyelle, Mr. (Francis Deloche de Noyelle), 117–19, 131, 133, 135, 141, 144, 188n1
Nun Kun, 161–65
Nuptse, 77
Nu-Te, 76
Nyima, 77

Oaku, 26, 45–47
Odling, Mrs., 67–68, 169
Okhaldhunga, 21, 40
Oliver, Mr., 68
Ondi, 41
Osmaston, Major, 95–96
Oudot, Jacques, 120

Palace of Justice, 98
Paldorje, 36
Palung, 31
Pangboche, 34–35
Pang-karma, 36
Pang-Kho-Ma, 76
Panglep Col, 69
Panmah Glacier, 111
Pansy, 123, 128–29, 138, 140, 145, 150
Paris, 153–59
Pasang, Ang, 46, 56, 184n2
Pathankot, 161
Pathans, 105
Paul, Karma, 53–55, 61, 66, 83
Pemionche, 48, 92
personality, 12
Phalut, 91
Phari, 50
Phar-ka-wa, 35
phemar, 38
Pheriche, 76
Pherinji, 110

Phi-nasa, 36
Phutar, Agu Pasang, 10
Phutar, Ang, 22
Phutar, Pasang, 42, 65, 182n5
Pierre, Bernard, 161, 165, 174
Porchi, 34–35
Pumori, 37, 55, 76, 78, 182n1, 186n21
Putliket, 148

Rai, 26
Rainplu, 62
Rakaposhi, 48
Rana, G. B., 122–23, 147
Ranighat, 123
Ranikhet, 83, 89, 96
Rauhul, Mr., 117–18
Rawalpindi, 99
Raxaul, 78, 150
Rébuffat, Gaston, 120, 129, 137, 140–41, 143
religion, 36
Rhamani, 84
Rhenok, 28
Richingpong, 92
Riddiford, Harold Earle, 74
Rin Nal, 162
Rinjin, 62
Rinsing, 42, 65
Rishi Ganga, 84, 88, 96
Rome, 154
Rongbuk, 54, 58, 62, 65, 72, 131
Rongbuk Glacier, 55, 63, 70
Rongbuk Monastery, 43, 131
Rongsher River, 78
roxi, 100
Russell, Scott, 112
Ruttledge, Hugh, 14, 40–42, 51, 53, 58–60, 64, 179

Sa La Mebar, 132
Sahib, Bara, 125–26, 130, 133, 135–38, 140–41, 143–48, 150–51, 156, 158, 161, 163–65
Sahib, Michel, 163–64
Sahib, Schatz, 127
sahibs, 62–63, 66, 68–69, 71, 75, 77–78, 84–87, 89, 92–93, 98–99, 101, 103–04, 109, 111, 117, 120–25, 128–32, 137, 140, 145, 147–50
Sar, 60–62
Sarki, 120–22, 128, 135–36,

138, 140, 145, 148, 188n3
Sarpo Laggo valley, 107
Satopanth Glacier, 85
Schabarth, G., 91
Schatz, Marcel, 120, 131, 140–44, 146, 155
Selu-La-Tu, 49
Shabre Subra, 54
Shaksgam River, 107
Shaksgam valley, 102, 109
Sha-la-ka, 36
Shangri-La, 8
Sharmi Lo, 29
Shekar Dzong, 21, 64–65, 69
Sherpa, Kami, 164
Sherpanis, 42
Shigar, 100
Shigatsé, 61
Shimshal col, 105–06
Shipton, Eric, 14, 33–34, 43, 53, 59, 61–62, 67–68, 70–71, 74, 76–78, 83, 87–89, 95–99, 102–06, 109, 112, 168–71, 179, 184n4
Shire, 36
sho-khang, 65
Shokta, 78
shortcomings, 12–13
Shugar, 78
Shyam-gup, 36
sickness, 26–27, 29
Sikkim, 28, 43, 51, 62, 64, 175
Siliguri, 151
Simina, 47–48
Singalapa, 47
Singalila, 91
Singlik, 63
Singtam, 49
Siri, William, 181n3
Sitar, Kusang, 185n13
Skardu, 100
smoking, 24–25
Smythe, F. S., 71, 171
snow blindness, 140–41
Solang, 47
Solba ridge, 47
Solu, 34–35
Solu-Khumbu, 21, 34, 40, 63–64, 73, 157
Somervell, Howard, 40
Sona Dhanga, 89
Song, Ang, 49
Sore, 35
Srinagar, 43, 99, 107, 109, 112, 165
stonemasons, 23

Sun Kosi, 34
Surkey, 76

Taj Mahal, 97
Taj Mahal Hotel, 98
Taksindu, 40
Tamur River, 47
Tansing, 122, 149–50
Tarahal col, 107
Tarikhel, 122
Tashi Dzong, 58, 69–70
Tashparu, 162, 165
Temba, Ang, 42, 183n10
Temba, Phur, 65, 71
Tempa, Nima, 48
Templa, 76
Temple of Fire, 131
Tengboche, 34–35, 76, 78
Tengboche Monastery, 21, 23, 26, 76
Tengkey Dzong, 54
Tengri Dzong, 69
Tenzing, Agu, 10
Tenzing, Lhakpa, 102–03, 104, 188n5
Tenzing, Sen, 95–98
te-ra-wa, 70
Terhathum, 47
terma, 38
Terray, Lionel, 120, 127, 131, 133, 137, 140–41, 146
testimonials, 167–74
Thakto, 36
Thame, 34, 78
Thami Khola, 35
Thamserku, 37
Thang Lung, 60
Thanggu, 63, 68
Thari, Ang, 92, 187n1
Tharkay, Agu, 7, 10
Tharkay, Ang, 9, 11–13, 130, 141, 145
Tharkay, Ching, 42
Tharkay, Fou, 120–23, 128–30, 188n3
Tharkay, Nim, 29, 45
Tharkay, Tsering, 57, 62, 65–66, 185n8
Thiningaon, 129
Thobuche, 37
Thondup, Dawa, 120–21, 130–31, 146, 149–50, 188n3
Thu, Mingma Thu, 48, 50, 184n3
Thumba, Nima, 42
Tibet, 29–32, 59, 61

Tibetan New Year, 25, 38
Tibetan Plateau, 8
Tilicho Col, 120, 129
Tilly, T. H., 184n13
Tilman, H.W., 14, 48, 68, 70–71, 73, 76, 83–84, 88, 95, 104–5, 179
Tista, 72
Tista River, 50
Togo, 168
Tom's Serac, 77
Tragbal col, 109
trees, 37
Tringtchuk, 128
tsampa, 38
Tsering, Ang, 42, 57, 64–66, 120–21, 123, 150, 183n9, 188n3, 189n1. *See also* Pansy
Tsering, Da, 42, 57, 65
Tsering, Yu, 77
Tukucha, 120, 124–25, 127, 131, 133, 189n2
Tumlingtar, 47
Tumsang, 50

Ukhimar, 87
Upon That Mountain, 14, 62, 104, 184n4, 185n5

Victoria Hospital, 48, 51
Victory on Annapurna, 153
village council, 39–40
Vittoz, Pierre, 161

Wager, Laurence Rickard, 57
Ward, Dr., 78
water, 25
wedding, 38–39
Wien, Wilhelm, 183n12
wife, 27
Wilson, Maurice, 62–63
Wood, D. F., 172

yak, 36
yam-dam, 38
Yarkand, 102–04
Yatung, 28, 50
Yerdzang, 38
Yeti, 78, 92, 97
Yuk-pa, 36

Zaz Nal, 162
Zemu Glacier, 49
Zimba, 76
Zoji La, 100

ABOUT THE AUTHOR

Born in 1908 ANG THARKAY was one of the leading Sherpas of the exploration period of the Himalaya. He was a regular on expeditions by Eric Shipton as well as sirdar for the successful French ascent of Annapurna. He was also on the 1951 Everest Reconnaissance – the trip in which Shipton met Hillary thus leading to Hillary's place on the 1953 team. Ang Tharkay opened his own guiding service in 1954, taking trekkers up Kangchenjunga, although he also continued to work for some high-level mountaineering expeditions. He died, of cancer, in 1981 in Kathmandu.

TASHI SHERPA is founder and CEO of Sherpa Adventure Gear, and the nephew of Ang Tharkay. His writing about the treatment and perception of Sherpas by Western climbers has appeared in *Alpinist* magazine.

DAWA SHERPA is the son of Ang Tharkay. He lives in Paris, France.

CORINNE MCKAY is an American Translators Association-certified French to English translator based in Boulder, Colorado. She has served as President of the Colorado Translators Association and was elected to a three-year term on the Board of Directors of the American Translators Association.

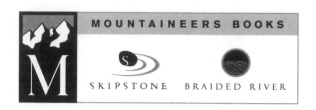

MOUNTAINEERS BOOKS is a leading publisher of mountaineering literature and guides—including our flagship title, *Mountaineering: The Freedom of the Hills*—as well as adventure narratives, natural history, and general outdoor recreation. Through our two imprints, Skipstone and Braided River, we also publish titles on sustainability and conservation. We are committed to supporting the environmental and educational goals of our organization by providing expert information on human-powered adventure, sustainable practices at home and on the trail, and preservation of wilderness.

The Mountaineers, founded in 1906, is a 501(c)(3) nonprofit outdoor recreation and conservation organization whose mission is to enrich lives and communities by helping people "explore, conserve, learn about, and enjoy the lands and waters of the Pacific Northwest and beyond." One of the largest such organizations in the United States, it sponsors classes and year-round outdoor activities throughout the Pacific Northwest, including climbing, hiking, backcountry skiing, snowshoeing, camping, kayaking, sailing, and more. The Mountaineers also supports its mission through its publishing division, Mountaineers Books, and promotes environmental education and citizen engagement. For more information, visit The Mountaineers Program Center, 7700 Sand Point Way NE, Seattle, WA 98115-3996; phone 206-521-6001; www.mountaineers.org; or email info@mountaineers.org.

Our publications are made possible through the generosity of donors and through sales of more than 600 titles on outdoor recreation, sustainable lifestyle, and conservation. To donate, purchase books, or learn more, visit us online:

MOUNTAINEERS BOOKS
1001 SW Klickitat Way, Suite 201 • Seattle, WA 98134
800-553-4453 • mbooks@mountaineersbooks.org • www.mountaineersbooks.org

THE LEGENDS AND LORE SERIES honors the lives and adventures of mountaineers and is made possible in part through the generosity of donors. Mountaineers Books, a nonprofit publisher, further contributes to this investment through book sales from more than 600 titles on outdoor recreation, sustainable lifestyle, and conservation.

We would like to thank the following for their charitable support of Legends and Lore:

FOUNDERS CIRCLE
- Anonymous
- Tina Bullitt
- Bill Buxton
- Tom and Kathy Hornbein*
- Hope and Dave Maltz
- Dianne Roberts and Jim Whittaker
- William Sumner
- Lawrence True and Linda Brown
- Doug and Maggie Walker

SUPPORTERS
- Byron Capps
- Roger Johnson
- Joshua Randow
- Jolene Unsoeld

With special appreciation to Tom Hornbein, who donates to the series all royalties earned through the sale of his book, Everest: The West Ridge.

You can help us preserve and promote mountaineering literature by making a donation to the Legends and Lore series. For more information, benefits of sponsorship, or how you can support future work, please contact us at mbooks@mountaineersbooks.org or visit us online at www.mountaineersbooks.org.

**MOUNTAINEERS
BOOKS**

The Legends and Lore series was created by Mountaineers Books in order to ensure that mountain literature will continue to be widely available to readers everywhere. From mountaineering classics to biographies of well-known climbers, and from renowned high-alpine adventures to lesser-known accomplishments, the series strives to bring mountaineering knowledge, history, and events to modern audiences in print and digital form.

Distinctive stories in the Legends and Lore series include:

My Father, Frank: The Forgotten Alpinist
Tony Smythe
This biography of Frank Smythe, written by his son, is "[t]imely, well-researched and written with the authority of a committed climber." –Doug Scott

That Untravelled World: An Autobiography
Eric Shipton
"You can't separate the fast-and-light aesthetic from the wry, ironic, understated brilliance of Shipton and Tilman's narratives . . . No glory for the fatherland bullshit, no 'first British ascent'—just good days in the mountains with friends." –David Roberts

Everest 1953: The Epic Story of the First Ascent
Mick Conefrey
"An exciting, moving account . . . a fascinating piece of documentary writing as readable and as poignant as *Into Thin Air* or *Touching the Void*."–*Spectator* (London)

Through a Land of Extremes:
The Littledales of Central Asia
Elizabeth and Nicholas Clinch
The life and times of a largely forgotten Victorian couple who just happened to make some of the most amazing expeditions of their day, including nearly reaching the forbidden city of Lhasa.

Brotherhood of the Rope:
The Biography of Charles Houston
Bernadette McDonald
Charlie Houston was an authentic American hero, famous not only for his role in the 1953 attempt on K2 but also for his pioneering research on the effects of high altitude.

MOUNTAINEERS
BOOKS